Starting from a Walk

Ron Wilson
Everdon Field Study Centre

with an Introduction by
Hugh Boulter
Director, World Education Service

Ilustrations by
Carol Boulter

Trentham Books

Introduction for Starting from a Walk

Charlotte Mason is remembered nowadays for the teacher training college which she founded in Ambleside, Cumbria and for the World-wide Education Service of the PNEU which specialises in the education of the children of English-speaking expatriates all over the world. The PNEU (Parents' National Education Union) was founded by Miss Mason in Bradford in 1897 and was initially an organisation which, through its various branches, encouraged parents to become involved in the education of their children.

However, Charlotte Mason saw herself as an educational thinker quite as much as an organiser. She laid great emphasis on first hand observation. "It seems to me a sine qua non of a living education that all school children of whatever grade should have one half-day in the week, throughout the year, in the fields. The teachers are careful not to make these nature walks an opportunity for scientific instruction, as we wish the children's attention to be given to observation with very little direction" (*School Education* pp.237, Kegan Paul, Trench, Trubner & Co Ltd). Charlotte Mason's ideas on observation and child-directed activity were certainly forward-thinking, not to say original, for her time and as with many of her ideas are easily incorporated in to the best of modern educational practice. In line with this the PNEU's World-Wide Education Service has been anxious to try to adapt her ideas for use today. Much of our work nowadays is with families living in remote places literally all over the world. Often the families are using our materials and professional support service to educate their children themselves. Sometimes the education takes place in small, two or three class schools attached to a hydro-electric scheme or an agricultural project. The difficulty lies not so much in the ideas as in their application. Charlotte Mason writes about squirrels, larch trees, jays and ground ivy which are totally applicable to the English Lake District but don't fit into the Libyan desert or the tropical rain forest of Indonesia.

So, whilst wishing to encourage environmental studies, we were hampered by very severe constraints in that our families and schools could be, literally, anywhere in the world. We were clearly not going to find any ready-made material to suit our purpose so we approached Ron Wilson of Everdon Field Study Centre, Northamptonshire to write a series of themes or topics for us. The outcome is "Starting from a Walk". The "Walk" in question is, of course, Charlotte Mason's nature walk, but in practice it does not necessarily require the half a day "in the fields" per week which she recommends. Nor is it possible to do all topics literally anywhere in the world. However, the emphasis is very much on the human body, the soil, the weather, the sky, the flora and the fauna — things which are observable in most places. The results have sometimes been exotic: for example, one eight year old in Kenya wrote: "I watched the poinsettias behind the old Kibor house and I saw several insects visiting the flowers. I saw two bees, lots of ants, and one unknown insect — it had a short, fat body with red and black/blue stripes, and wins. It was attacking the ants". Expatriates often bemoan the problems of education overseas but there can be advantages too. Indeed, "Starting from a Walk" has given so much pleasure to our families and schools world-wide that we felt that it deserved a wider market in the United Kingdom; hence our approach to Trentham Books and this publication.

Hugh Boulter
Director WES/PNEU

Starting From A Walk

Ron Wilson
Head of Everdon Field Centre, Northamptonshire

Introduction by Hugh Boulter, Director of the World-wide Education Service

Illustrated by Carol Boulter

Trentham Books Ltd.,
151 Etruria Road,
Stoke-on-Trent, ST1 5NS

© World-wide Education Service/Parents' National Education Unit 1988

All rights reserved. No part of this publication may be reproduced, stored in retrieval system, or transmitted in any form or by any means, electronic, mechanical, photocopying, recording or otherwise, without the prior permission of Trentham Books.

Set and printed in Great Britain by:
Bemrose Press Ltd./Cheshire Typesetters, Chester.

Cover design reproduced by kind permission of
Start-rite Shoes Ltd., Norwich.

Introduction

Starting from a Walk — Introduction

Because we live in such a sophisticated age, with its wealth of technology, its computers and its microchips, which have sought if not to control, at least to manipulate our lives, we have often lost sight of the simple things. It is too easy to forget, or even dismiss, the natural world, the environment around us, as a mere triviality or irrelevance.

But, as it is very important to remember, it forms an important part of our lives. Whilst the term 'environmental awareness' might seem like a phrase dreamt up by the advertiser, nevertheless, we do need to seek inspiration from, and come to terms with, our environment in the true Charlotte Mason tradition. Moreover, we need our environment. We need the plants to make food, because we cannot do it; we need the soil to grow our crops in, and we need all of nature to add aesthetically to our often mundane lives.

There is a wealth of interest in our environment. We share our planet with other living things, both plant and animal. We gain great inspiration from such simple pleasures as a tree bursting into leaf or a flower into bloom.

We felt that since we have so much around us, we should make use of it. But we also felt that it would be wrong to divorce ourselves from nature. Too often man has considered himself apart from his environment, rather than a part of it.

With this in mind we have planned our environmental studies project STARTING FROM A WALK, which will enable us to begin our studies outside, but also to look at those parts of us which we use to be able to carry out our studies.

In writing this project we have had to incorporate certain guidelines so that we could give as much help as possible to parents. This may sound very rigid, but it is not meant to be. We hope that as parents become involved with this material, they will take advantage of what is happening around them. Listen to the questions your children ask. From these there could be easy leads into some of the follow-up material. Even if a question does not give rise to an activity, there may be other things which you could do.

Watch your surroundings — use changes in them — e.g. sandstorms, the rainy season, snowy season, rises and falls of temperature, changes of season.

Practice keeping your ears and mind open. Make use of **your** surroundings. We can only offer suggestions, because we do not know exactly what your location is like.

Preliminary

Of course it is possible to get most of the material which we talk about second-hand from books. However, it will be more interesting and more fun if you can carry out the investigations.

Most of us walk at some time or other. It might be a regular long walk, or even a short walk. Sometimes it might be for a specific purpose — to the shop or the post office — or for pleasure.

We thought that one of the best ways of encouraging children to observe what is around them would be to take them on a regular walk. This might sound rather mundane when put like that. But, as you follow the suggestions about what to do, we hope that you will become excited about it. If you walk along the same route regularly over a period of time, you will be able to discover the changes which take place. Some of these might be minor: others might be major.

There are many activities which can ensure that the walk is interesting while you are doing it. But we realise that there might be problems in some environments, and to help overcome this we have divided the project into two sections.

There are those activities which will be prompted by the walk, and which will teach your child more about the world around him/her. There are also activities which make the walk possible, worthwhile and enjoyable. The use of the eyes and ears, for example. We give you a large number of follow-up activities to choose from (the assignments).

To enable you to carry out these investigations they have been set out in the form of assignment sheets. We have used a diagram overleaf — concentric approach — to show how they relate to the main theme. There is a large number of assignment sheets to enable you to choose follow-up activities.

As you get to know your walk, you will be able to devise some of your own activities, like simply I-spy quizzes. During the week you will be spending some time on the walk and writing up any observations and about 2 hours on the follow-up activities.

How do we start? We all have a problem: we forget things! To make sure that your weekly walk is accurately recorded, you will need some equipment.

Introduction

GENERAL ACTIVITIES

12, 13, 19, 47, 49

Introduction

What you need

1 Field notebook — this should be hard back and measure about 100mm x 160mm. This size will easily slip into a pocket. This book should be used on the walk. It should also be used by the child at other times to record 'natural' observations. This will be a useful notebook to be used between walks as well.

2 Clipboard and paper. A small clipboard — about 25cm x 20cm is necessary. It can be used by the children to make drawings, and be taken out for artwork.

3 Paints — a small paintbox which can be taken out for the child to record impressions at regular intervals.

4 Collecting bags — for collecting 'bits and pieces' on the way.

5 Small haversack — for carrying things — clipboard, identification books, etc.

6 Hand lens — with string tied to it, so that it can hang around the neck.

7 Camera — a Polaroid camera is a worthwhile investment, perhaps as a Christmas or birthday present. You can arrange to take a photograph each week as you walk. You could do this in one of two ways. You could either take a photograph of the same thing — e.g. a tree — or at the same spot, each week. Whatever you do, it will provide a useful, visual stimulus. It will bring back memories, and can be used for other work.

8 Large hardback book — 25cm x 20cm. This is useful for writing up the information collected on the walk. If you ensure that the drawing paper is the same size, you could stick this in at an appropriate place. (Some people find a loose-leaf file is better for this part of the work. There are advantages and disadvantages in both systems, and I think that it is a matter of personal choice.)

How to choose the walk

You will need to choose as interesting a walk as possible. Your walk should be at least 1km long, but the length will depend on the ability of your child. You and your child should walk the same route at least once a week.

Of course the questions to be asked are, "What makes the walk interesting?" or "How do I choose an interesting walk?"

Let's look at the first question. What might be interesting for one person, might not be for another! We can only give some guidelines.

Since you are going to have to go over the same walk every week for the next year, there needs to be plenty to see! If there are any trees, other plants, birds, butterflies, insects etc., there should be enough for the child to see and become interested.

Introduction

You could choose the route of the walk on your own. You could do this by making a number of walks. Look for interesting sights along the way. If there are trees, can you discover whether there are any animals living in them? Look out for flowers. Choose areas where there are bright and colourful ones if possible. These will attract the child's attention. If you have water — a stream or a river bank — so much the better. Water attracts wildlife, and it is always popular with youngsters. It could also be useful if you decide to go tracking (see Assignment sheet 48), because there are usually animal footprints left in soft mud.

When you have been on a few walks you could take your child along them all. Let him/her decide which is the most interesting. You will often find that the aspects which you thought were good, might not be of interest to your child. Never despair, thank goodness we all have different tastes!

When to go for the walk
You might wonder what is the best time of the day to go on your walk. It will depend on where you live. Certain times of the day are often more interesting and exciting than others. The age of your child, the day's temperatures etc, will determine your decision. To start with you could try going for your walk — with your child — at various times. You should be able to decide which is the more interesting. Plant life will generally not vary its activities as much as animals. Plants do close their flowers at different times of the day in certain atmospheric conditions.

Keeping Records
Keeping records is an important aspect of any activity. There are arguments for and against either keeping rigid records — i.e. having a set format, or what I sometimes refer to as 'haphazard arrangements'. In the former there is a set pattern, in the latter there isn't. Let's look at the first method.

The reason for keeping records is at least two-fold. Firstly, we want to encourage children to use their eyes and discover what is going on around them. Secondly, we want to be able to look back over our weekly walks, so that we can compare what has been happening. It is easier to do this if weekly records are the same. Thus we suggest that each entry (and we suggested earlier that the notebook can be used for other natural observations besides the walk) should have:

Date
Time of walk (try and keep it to about the same time each week)
Weather (for further details of keeping regular records see Assignment sheets 1-7).
Details of observations

You might find the following example of how your child might set out his/her field notebook useful.

> Monday January 18th
> 10.30 a.m.
> Weather: Sunny, a few clouds. Cool. (5°C)
> Very muddy. snow has melted.
> Bluetits in Lilac bush? How many pairs are there?
> Sycamore buds swollen, brought a twig home.
> Path to stream has broken up. Why — is it the ice?
> Stream nearly up to its banks and very muddy. How do fish survive?
> Chestnuts eaten by squirrel at foot of sweet chestnut tree. Found some prickly cases 100 paces from the tree.

Each observation should be written down as it is seen. You might have to write them down for the young child. If you do, please ensure that you write down what the child wants you to! It is very tempting to write down your own observations. You could carry your own notebook, too, and keep your own natural records. This is useful because you will undoubtedly see things which your child doesn't, and vice versa. This makes for a useful comparison at the end of the walk.

There is a tendency to write down the minimum of information. For example a child will write,

'Eagle seen'

However, try to encourage the child to discover as much as possible about the 'eagle'.

Where was it (in this case the eagle)?
What was it doing?
Were there any other animals about?
Have you seen it before?
If so, when?

You may find the child cannot answer the question, 'What was it doing?' because there might not be any visible signs. You might need to rephrase the question, 'Can you think of anything which it might have been doing?'

There are other ideas which you might consider worthwhile.

1 Let the child choose a number of spots on each walk, and tell you why he/she found them exciting and especially interesting.

2   You choose a few stops on the walk. The number will depend on your child. Up to five should be ideal. You could stop at each one and make detailed observations. We can only give you an example. Supposing there is a tree. Look at it closely on each visit (see Assignment sheet 26 for further details).

You could then make a large drawing of a tree. Buds, leaves, flowers, fruits and animals associated with the tree could be cut out, and stuck on. This will give the child some idea that the tree is not a 'solitary' object, but a living thing, and important for many other forms of wildlife.

3   You might consider letting your child make a map of your walk. You will need the recording board for this. Let them draw the map as they go along. You can work with them. But let the child also decide what he/she wants to include — they have a much more interesting sense of priorities than adults! We have shown an example of a map below:

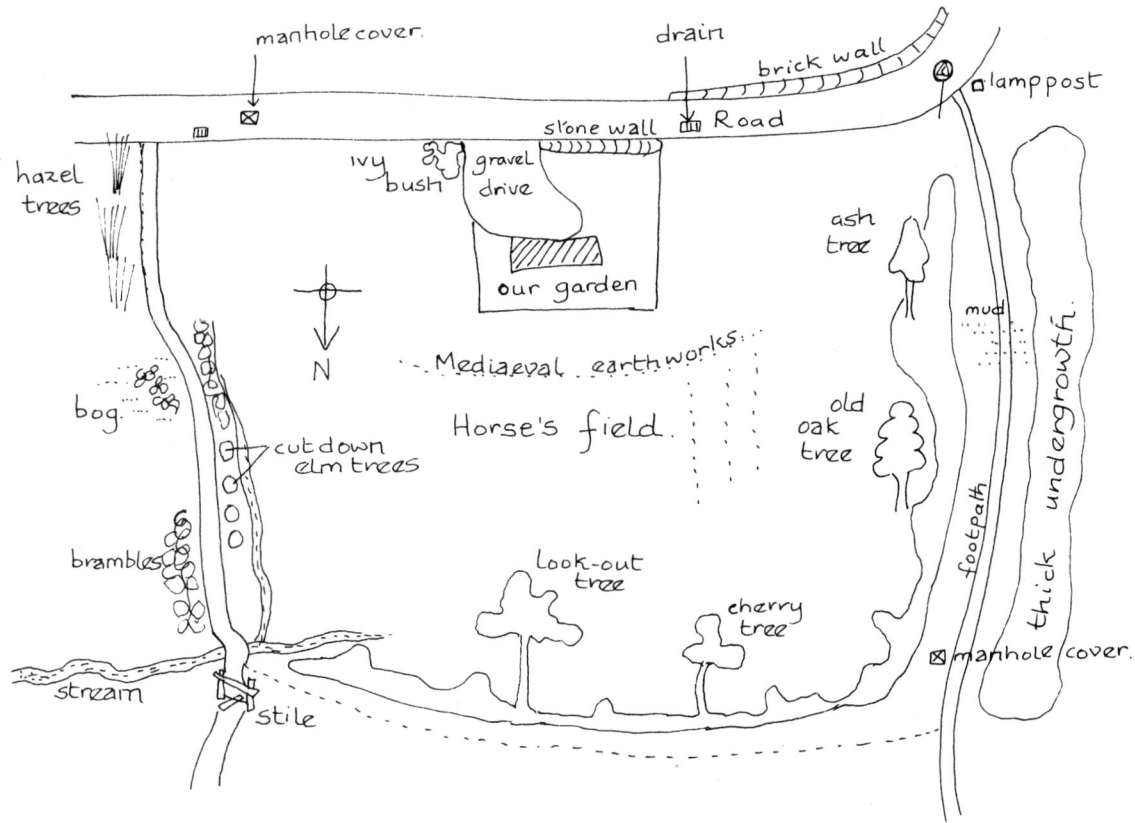

Introduction

4   It is a good idea to let your child make his own nature trail. He will then be able to show it to other people who will be able to use it. The 'answer' which other people get to any 'questions' will prove useful to the child — again for comparisons.

5   Children always want to collect things. Encourage them to respect the countryside around them, whatever it is like. Collections can be made, but preferably of things which they find have been 'discarded'. They might be pieces of bark which have fallen off trees, twigs which have snapped off, plants which have been nibbled, food left by aniamls — nuts, etc. This is all very useful follow up work (Assignment sheet 48).

After the walk
Having returned home laden with notes, information etc., what do you do with it?

The observations should be talked about some more, if need be. They might have asked questions which have not yet been answered. Keep details of questions posed whilst out. For example, 'What does the eagle eat?' These should be answered as soon as possible after the walk. The first priority, therefore, is to deal with the walk material.

It is useful to let the child write up (or have written up, using his words) his notes in the larger notebook or looseleaf file. Any Polaroid photographs taken should be mounted with the notes. Sketches can also be included here.

Take the recording board paper and paints with you, at least once a month, so that your child can record his/her impressions. What to paint should not be a problem. It might be a scene, or a particular flower or tree. It doesn't matter, as long as your child is recording **his/her** impressions on **his/her** walk.

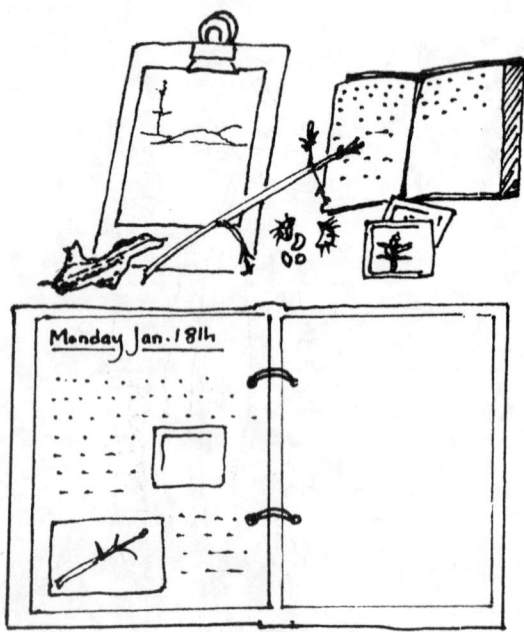

Children should be encouraged to illustrate their notes. They might have made sketches whilst they were out, or can use reference books for reference purposes to assist them. Don't encourage them simply to copy illustrations from books.

THE ASSIGNMENTS

The Assignment Sheets
From each walk information will be amassed, so that, hopefully, in a short time there will be a geat deal of information. We want to build on this basic information in our assignments.

There is material in each assignment for two levels — Primary 3 and 4 and Primary 5 and 6. If you are new to the projects, then carry out Primary 3 and 4 first, even if your child is at Primary 5 and 6. This is important because some Primary 5 and 6 will make very little sense unless the previous assignment has been attempted. You will see from the list of Assignments that there are 78 sheets in all, but you will find that you will probably only work from about 26 each year. In this way there will be enough in the pack for you to use for your years' work.

On each sheet we have used two symbols. **P** indicates that the parent should read that part of the card, and if it contains some hint of an answer to an assignment, try not to let the child see it until the end.

C indicates that the child should read that passage.

P & C indicates that both parent and child should read this section together, before starting the investigation. Alternatively, some children can read it on their own. They should be allowed to do this, provided that the parent has already read it, has the materials, and understands the procedure. The parent will also need to be around so that the child can be given any help with (a) the reading, and (b) the investigation. The latter is especially important, as you will see, since some of the activities can only be carried out by the child and parent together.

It is a good idea to become involved with your child in these activities, and to take part as fully as possible. In some investigations, for example, we suggest that 'It would be a good idea if you both (i.e.) parent and child) did this'.

There are two groups of assignments 'What we saw on the Walk' and 'What we used on the Walk'.

How do you decide which assignment to select? This isn't an easy question to answer, because we would hope that parents would be able to choose those which have resulted from something encountered on the walk.

While you are reading this section look again at the concentric circle diagram and see how the assignments relate to each other.

1 What we used on the Walk
Some parents will have difficulty in following the walk on a regular basis, if they live in areas which do not have much wild life to observe. We also feel that, whilst dealing with what the child discovers, we should also look at the child himself and what parts of himself he uses to go on the walk and make observations.

Perhaps we could give you an example from this section. You might ask your child what they used to discover the colour of flowers. Hopefully the answer would be eyes! You would then be able to select Assignment sheet 66 and/or Assignment sheet 71.

2 What we saw on the Walk
This set consists of a number of assignments which can be initiated either during a walk, or as a result of observations made on that walk. An assignment might be directly concerned with one aspect of the walk, such as further studies of a tree (Assignment sheet 26), or it might be keeping stick insects (Assignment sheet 22). In the case of the latter, observations can be made so that the child (and parent) can discover more about the activities of one particular group of insects.

You might find seeds whilst out on your walk. It would be a good idea to grow some of these. You will find that there is an Assignment (sheet 38), which deals with growing seeds.

In order to help parents as much as possible with the assignments we have set out all the sheets in the same way.

Length of time needed
The length of time necessary to complete an assignment has many variables. It will depend (a) on the assignment and (b) on the child. As we mention later some assignments can be completed in a single session — those on sight, for example. Others have to be set up and left for some time. Those on growing things fall into this category.

Materials needed
At the beginning of each assignment you will find details of all the materials you need to collect together before you start. This is under the heading: **You will need.** This should be useful, because you will be able to see at a glance whether you have all the items or whether you need to obtain any.

Introduction

When selecting the Assignments we have chosen projects which, on the whole, do not need a great deal of equipment, because we realise that many people might have problems. Where we have suggested various items it is often possible to look around the house/school and improvise. As long as what we are using works that is all that matters. If at all possible, you could try to find alternatives for the equipment we suggest so that you are not prevented altogether from doing the experiments.

Keeping records

Just as we have found it important to make careful observations and record them on our walks, we need to keep records for our indoor follow-up activities.

You can use the field notebook for record-keeping, or you could have a similar book (160mm x 100mm) which can be kept specially for recording details of the investigations.

Any investigation has a sequence thus:
- What we do and why we do it
- How we do it
- What we discovered (found out) from the investigation
- What we can say about our discovery

It is important that even when an investigation did not work out, the study should still be recorded.

Although we have suggested that the sequence discussed above should be followed, it is important that the child be allowed to make records about his/her investigations in his/her own words, using simple plain English.

Suffice it to say that drawings can be used where these help — and they are often suggested in the investigations. The child's conclusions — which can also include drawings — should be written up in everyday English.

It is important that the child gets into the habit of regular and careful recording. Some of the investigations will be completed in a single session, but others will have to be set up, and then investigated over a period of time. The value of careful record-keeping cannot be over-estimated in this case.

As long as the sequence mentioned above is followed, the way in which records are kept will vary from individual to individual. The age and ability of the child will also be factors which must be considered. But a drawing — of apparatus in particular — is often much more valuable than 'reams' of carefully written notes. When looking at the records of an investigation both parent and child should be able to understand exactly what has been done, and what 'results' have been obtained.

Assessment

Obviously parents want to know how their children are coping with the project material, and what they are learning from it. Although each Assignment sheet is aimed at eliciting a different response from the child, nevertheless, we have devised a format which we hope will benefit both child and parent.

The following notes will help parents to assess their child's progress:

1 **The walk**

What sort of questions are the children asking:

a) at the start of the environmental studies project:
b) after a few weeks
and
c) at the end of a year?

For example, has their awareness of a tree on the walk increased? It is a good idea to keep a record of their questions in your own field notebook. Compare the questions asked over a period of time.

Do they ask 'Is it a butterfly?' still or do they become more involved by putting deeper questions like, 'Why is that butterfly where it is?' or 'Where does the butterfly lay its eggs?' or 'Why do we see butterflies at some times of the year and not others?'

Look carefully at what they are recording whilst on the walk. Do they notice things and record them? Do you still have to 'prompt' them? Can they make their own 'guesses' when they pose a question? Can they go to books to look up the information? Do they want to find out more?

2 **The Assignment Sheets**

As you will realise each Assignment sheet is laid out in the same way. Initially these may seem strange to children (and parents as well), but over a period of time the format will enable children to become familiar with them. This will aid them in their assignments.

Are they able to read and understand what they are meant to be doing? If they cannot read, are they able to understand from parent's instructions what they are meant to be doing?

Once they have understood the format, are they able to carry out the Assignments themselves as they progress? If they are still very much dependent on parents, then their progress is less evident than where youngsters are able to 'carry on'.

Can they set up the investigations?
Can they devise similar investigations?
Do they think of other problems as they go through the Assignments?

If a certain piece of equipment is not available do they make suggestions as to alternatives? In other words, can they improvise?
Do they question their results?
Do they suggest that it would be a good idea to repeat some of the investigations (a) again or (b) with other people?
Can they organise their own investigations?

Look back over their recording. Has this improved? Do they ask deeper questions? Do they query what they are doing? Do they query their results? Do they suggest that some results might be wrong? Do they suggest why this might be?

Can they devise other assignments/investigations to test problems which arise as a result of the work which they are doing?

ASSIGNMENT
NUMBER   TITLE   **Date completed**
1   Design a Weather Board
2   Looking at a Barometer — and Using One
3   Looking at Air Pressure
4   Measuring Humidity
5   Keeping Temperature Records
6   Recording Cloud Cover
7   Rainfall Records
8   Rain and Evaporation
9   Making and Using A Weather Vane
10   Finding Out About Shadows & Making a Shadow Clock
11   Looking at Leaf Litter
12   Starting a Collection
13   Making Simple Keys
14   Looking at Soil
15   Bird Feeding Project
16   What Seeds do Birds Like?
17   When Do Birds Come to Feed?
18   Bird Nesting Boxes
19   Make A Pooter
20   Looking At and Keeping Minibeasts
21   Finding Out About Insects
22   Keeping Stick Insects
23   Looking at Snails
24   Further Studies with Earthworms
25   Discover How Many Worms Live in Your Lawn
26   Adopt a Tree
27   Patterns in Bark
28   How Old is That Tree?
29   Looking at Leaves
30   Estimating and measuring Tree Heights
31   Keeping Small Mammals
32   One Square Metre
33   An Outdoor Plot
34   Looking at Flowers
35   Insect Visitors to Flowers
36   Looking at Seed Dispersal
37   Looking at Fruits and Seeds
38   Conditions for Seed Germination
39   Seeds Grow Towards the Light

Introduction

40	Looking at Bulbs Growing	....
41	Growing Potatoes	....
42	Growing Plants from Cuttings	....
43	Spores are Invisible	....
44	Growth in Twigs	....
45	Make a Sponge Garden	....
46	Looking at Life in Water	....
47	Setting up an Aquarium	....
48	Making Tracks	....
49	Plaster Casting	....
50	Looking at Cells	....
51	Looking at Frameworks	....
52	Tongue rolling and Tongue folding	....
53	Heights and Weights	....
54	How Quickly do we React?	....
55	How Our Arms and Legs Move	....
56	Listening to Sounds	....
57	Sounds from Hidden Objects	....
58	Hearing distances	....
59	How are sounds Caused?	....
60	Teeth and Feeding	....
61	Feeling Hot and Cold	....
62	Finding Out About Pain	....
63	Finding Out About Touch	....
64	More About Touch and Feel	....
65	Discover by Feel	....
66	Looking at Eyes	....
67	Looking at Colours	....
68	Seeing Colours	....
69	Do Our Eyes Deceive Us? (1)	....
70	Do Our Eyes Deceive Us? (2)	....
71	How Our Eyes Work	....
72	The Use of Lenses	....
73	Making a Flickergraph	....
74	Discovering whether certain areas of the tongue are sensitive to certain tastes	....
75	Taste and Smell	....
76	Smell Without Seeing	....
77	Looking at Different Faces	....
78	Looking at Differences — Fingerprints	....

Introduction

Book List

We have listed some reference sources. We have not attempted to list identification books. To do so would be impossible, because of the almost global nature of the World-Wide Education Service.

In addition to the reference books, we have also indicated those which will allow you to carry out further studies. Although these may mention 'British' species, the techniques can be adopted for use in other parts of the world.

You will find the numerous pamphlets published by the School Natural Science Society, and distributed by the Association for Science Education, College Lane, Hatfield, Herts, AL10 9AA, very useful. We have listed many of these. Although they are aimed at schools, the ideas expressed are simple and can be used in the home situation. In the list below (R) indicates a Reference book; (P) indicates a practical guide, with ideas for further study. Some books have both letters because they cover both categories.

Jennings, Terry. The Young Scientist Investigates Birds. Oxford (P).
Jennings, Terry. The Young Scientist Investigates Flowers. Oxford (P).
Jennings, Terry. The Young Scientist Investigates Seeds and Seedlings. Oxford (P).
Jennings, Terry. The Young Scientist Investigates Small Garden Animals. Oxford (P).
Jennings, Terry. The Young Scientist Investigates Trees. Oxford (P).
Wilson, Ron. The Nature Detective's Notebook. Knight (P).
Mossman, Keith. The Pip Book. Penguin (P).
Schöfper, Siegfried. The Young Specialist Looks at Weather. Burke (R/P).
Ashley, Bernard. Weather Men. Allman (R/P).
Hammersley, Alan. Weather and Life. Blandford (R/P).
Wilson, Ron. The Life of Plants. Ward Lock (R).
— Have Fun With Nature — Book 1. Macdonald (P).
— Have Fun With Nature — Book 2. Macdonald (P).
— Have Fun With Nature — Book 3. Macdonald (P).
— Have Fun With Nature — Book 4. Macdonald (P).
Blackford, Susan. Let's Investigate Trees. Blackie (P).
Blackford, Susan. Let's Investigate Birds. Blackie (P).
Blackford, Susan. Let's Investigate Insects. Blackie (P).
Wilson, Ron. Making a Collection. School Natural Science Society (P).
Hutchinson, Ken. Butterflies and Moths. Macmillan Education (P).
Hutchinson, Ken. Spiders. Macmillan Education (P).
Hutchinson, Ken. Ants. Macmillan Education (P).
Hutchinson, Ken. Pond Life. Macmillan Education (P).
Anderson, D and McQuillen, B. Mud, Daisies and Sparrows (Exploring Out-Door Environments). Studies in Education Ltd (R/P).

McKinley, Brian. Growing Things. Studies in Education Limited (R/P).
Arnold, Neil. Wildlife Conservation for Young People. Ward Lock Limited.
Crush, Margaret. Handy Homes for Creepy Crawlies. Dragon/Granada (P).
Shove, R F. Trees Cultivated in Pots. School Natural Science Society (P).
Bond, P M. Animal Tracks and Clues. School Natural Science Society (P).
Wootton, M J. Simple Experiments with Seeds and Seedlings. SNSS (P).
Quayle, N J. Concrete yard Garden with young Children. SNSS (P).
Gregory, V B A. The Keeping of Animals and Plants in School. SNSS (P).
Pugh E C. Earthworms. SNSS (P).
Finch, I E. Trees Their Form and Branching. SNSS (P).
Leutscher, A. Living Amphibians and Reptiles as Classroom Animals. SNSS (P).
Shaw, P B. Making Vivaria. SNSS (P).
Hollings, M. Living Amphibians and Reptiles as Classroom Animals. SNSS (P).
Finch I E. The Use of Identification Keys with Children. SNSS (P).
Leadley Brown, A M. Stick Insect. SNSS (R/P).
Caloe, Michael. Bird Flight. SNSS (R/P).
Tuke, E M. Snails and Slugs. SNSS (R/P).
Chinery, M. The Family Naturalist. Macdonald and Jane. (P).
Barnes, A. Practical Book of Pet Keeping. Crusade Against All Cruelty to Animals Ltd, Avenue Lodge, Bounds Green Road, London N22 4EU.
Stannard, Peter. Sense Systems (Man and Nature). Macmillan Education (R/P).
Riley, P D. Life Science. Groundwork in Biology. Hulton.
McKean, D G. Introduction to Biology. John Murray (R/P).
Finch, I. Science Workshop. Longmans (P).
Wilson, Ron. How the Body Works. Ward Lock (R).
Cornell, J B. Sharing Nature With Children. Exley Publications/Inter-Action (R/P).
Delaney, M R. Build Your Body. Macmillan Education (P).
—— The Optical Illusion Pad. John Adams Toys (P).
Catherall, Ed. Touch. Wayland (P/R).
Catherall, Ed. Taste and Smell. Wayland (P/R).
Ward, Brian R. Skeleton and Movement. F Watts (R).
Ward, Brian R. Ear and Hearing. F Watts (R).
Edlin, P. How to be a Detective. Beaver (P/R).

Ladybird Books produce a large number of titles. Many of these would be useful in this work. They also produce filmstrips, which can be cut into slides. These are based on the books. For a complete up-to-date catalogue, write to Ladybird Books, Loughborough, Leicestershire.

Assignment Number 1

Design A Weather Board

P & C As part of the weather project, it is a good idea to devise a weather board. This can be mounted in the work space. It is also a good useful idea to keep a monthly record sheet. If each is then filed safely the records can be compared from year to year.

You will need:
Piece of hardboard or thick card, pencils, etc for illustrating the weather board.

Do this
1 Organise your weather board so that you can show the following things each day:

        rainfall
        sun
        cloud cover
        wind speed

Use the symbols that we show or make up your own.

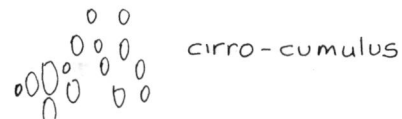 cirro-cumulus

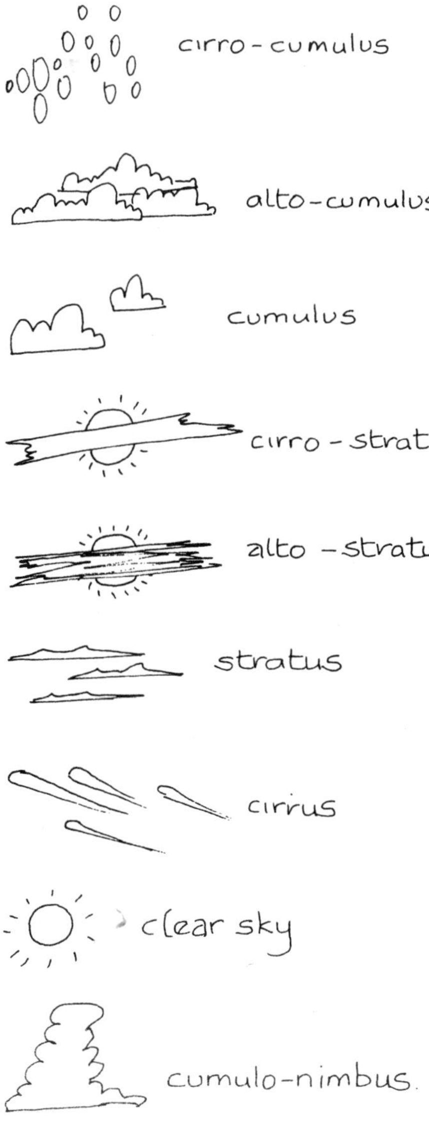

 alto-cumulus

 cumulus

 cirro-stratus

 alto-stratus

 stratus

 cirrus

 clear sky

2 Keep your weather board up to date.

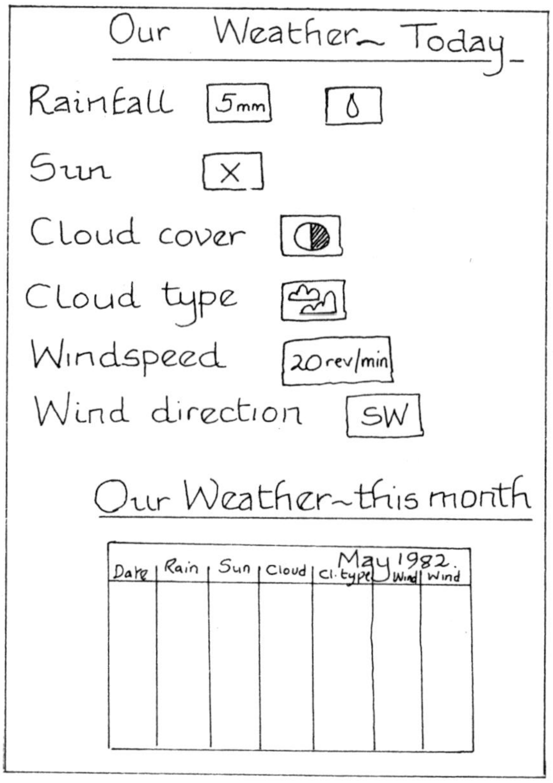

cumulo-nimbus.

Assignment Number 2

Looking at a Barometer — and Using One

P & C If you have a barometer in your house, you can record the readings regularly as part of the weather project. High pressure gives a settled period; low pressure unsettled conditions. Although we do not realise it is happening to us, air pressure changes constantly. It is around us all the time, and presses constantly on our bodies. There are changes in air pressure at various heights. The lowest air pressure is at the tops of mountains; the highest at sea level.

Primary 3 and 4
You will need:
Notebook, pencils, access to barometer.

Do this
1 Record the barometer readings each day — at about the same time
OR
2 Record the barometer readings when you get up and before you go to bed.

Think about this
1 At the end of each week look at your readings.

2 If you took readings twice a day, did you notice any differences during the day?

3 Did you notice any difference during the week?

4 If you keep records for a long time, you will be able to see some of the changes which take place through the seasons.

5 Did you notice what sort of weather it was when there was low pressure?
Did you notice what sort of weather it was when there was high pressure?

Primary 5 and 6
You can make your own simple barometer. This will show changes in air pressure.

You will need:
Milk bottle, piece of rubber (from a balloon, for example) elastic band, drinking straw, pieces of ply wood, graph paper, notebook, pencil.

Do this
1 Before you start, place the milk bottle on a radiator or in a window to warm it.

2 Use a piece of rubber from the balloon and stretch this over the top of the milk bottle, securing it with the elastic band.

3 Cut one end of the straw to a point.

4 Use glue to stick the other end to the centre of the rubber cover.

5 Join your two pieces of plywood together to form an L-shape.

6 Place the jar on the board, so that the straw is almost touching the back board.

7 Glue the jar in place.

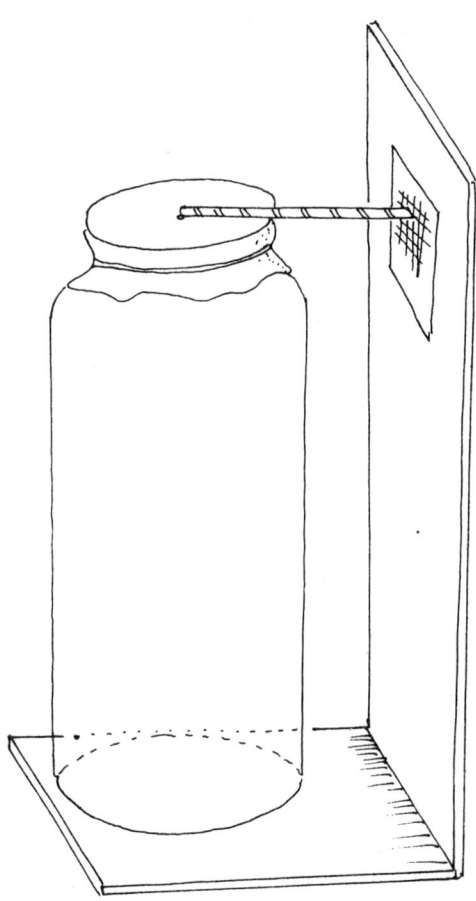

8 Attach a piece of graph paper to the board at the back.

9 As the air pressure changes, the straw will move up and down.

Look at your barometer each day, and mark on the graph paper the position of the straw and date.

Think about this
1 Were you able to record changes in air pressure?

2 Can you compare some of your other weather records — such as temperature, wind speeds, etc — with the changes in air pressure?

Find out more
1 Try and find out how air pressure is important in, for example, the canning industry.

2 Find out about air pressure of balloons and airships.

3 See if you can discover anything about the effects of changes in air pressure as pilots fly higher.

2a

Assignment Number 2

4 What effects does air pressure (or lack of it) have on such people as astronauts?

5 What makes your ears 'pop' when you go down a mine or into a tunnel at speed, such as in a train?

6 Can you think of other ways in which air pressure might affect you? ☐

Assignment Number 3

Looking at Air Pressure

P Because some phenomena are invisible they are often difficult to understand. Air pressure is one of these. However, we can show how it works with the use of a home-made barometer. There is a simple investigation to prove that there is air pressure.

C Air pressure cannot be seen, but we can carry out a simple investigation to show that it is present.

You will need:
Glass bottle, water, plasticine, straw, notebook, pencil.

Do this
1 Put some water in the bottle.
2 Put in the straw and suck up some water.
3 You probably find it quite easy. As you suck on the straw, you are pulling out water. Other air pushes down on the liquid, pushing it up the straw.

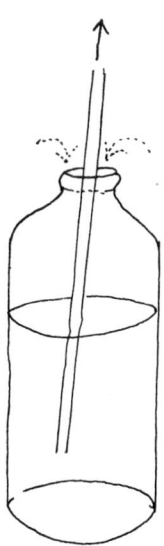

4 Make sure that your bottle is now only half full of water.

5 Put the straw in.

6 Seal the top completely with plasticine. Take care not to squash the straw.

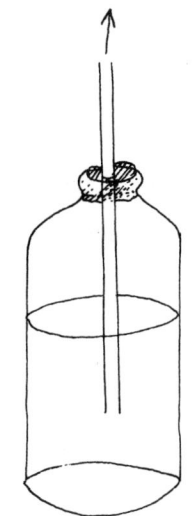

7 Now try sucking up the straw to draw up the liquid.

Think about this
1 What did you discover?

2 Can you explain why it was easier when the top of the bottle was not sealed?

Assignment Number 4

Measuring Humidity

P The amount of moisture in the air varies from day to day and from one part of the day to another. Moisture comes mainly from areas of water, like ponds, lakes and the sea. But it comes from plants as well. In woodlands, where there is a concentration of plants, there is usually more humidity than in the surrounding area. We do not see the water, because it is in the form of invisible water vapour. A simple piece of equipment will enable changes in the humidity to be seen.

C All around us all the time there is invisible water vapour. We call this humidity. We can carry out a simple investigation to show that it changes from time to time.

You will need:
Piece of card at least 30cm x 18cm, paper, scissors, a long human hair, sellotape, pin, your notebook, pencil.

Do this
1 Cut out two pieces of card. One should be 15cm x 12cm and the other 15cm x 6cm.

2 Attach the larger piece of card to the smaller piece to form a stand — rather like a picture frame.

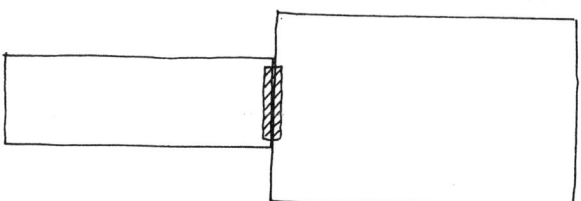

3 Cut out an arrow from the piece of plain paper.

4 Use the pin to attach the straight end of the arrow near to the bottom of the card.

5 Use sellotape to fix one end of the hair to the point of the arrow, and the other end to the card above the point.

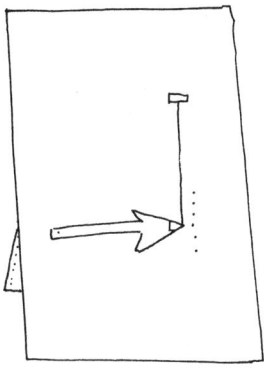

Think about this
1 Look at the card regularly.
2 See if you can see any changes in the hair/arrow.
3 Keep careful records.
4 Do you know why it is happening?

Assignment Number 5

Keeping Temperature Records

P & C As a complete package, the various information collected from your weather project will give a better picture of what is happening. Although in Primary 3 and 4 you will only be able to collect some information, once you get to Primary 5 and 6, you will be able to look more carefully at your records and draw some conclusions. We have already suggested some ways of doing this. Keeping temperature records is a valuable and important part of the weather project.

You will need:
Maximum and minimum thermometer, small notebook, pencil.

Do this
1 If you can make a Stevenson's screen to house your thermometer, so much the better. This is a box with slats around the front and sides to allow air to circulate freely. It should be placed in the open away from buildings for the best results.

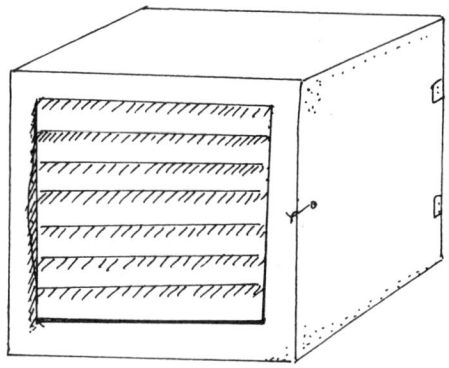

Stevenson's screen.

2 Take the maximum and minimum temperature at a regular time each day.

Primary 3 and 4
Think about this
1 When was it very hot?
2 When was it very cold?

Primary 5 and 6
Do this
1 Plot the temperatures on graph paper. Plot the maximum temperature in one colour and the minimum temperature in another colour.

Think about this
Look at your temperature graph.

1 On which day(s) was the greatest difference between maximum and minimum temperatures?
2 On which day(s) was the least difference between maximum and minimum temperatures?
3 Were there any days where the maximum and minimum temperatures remained about the same?

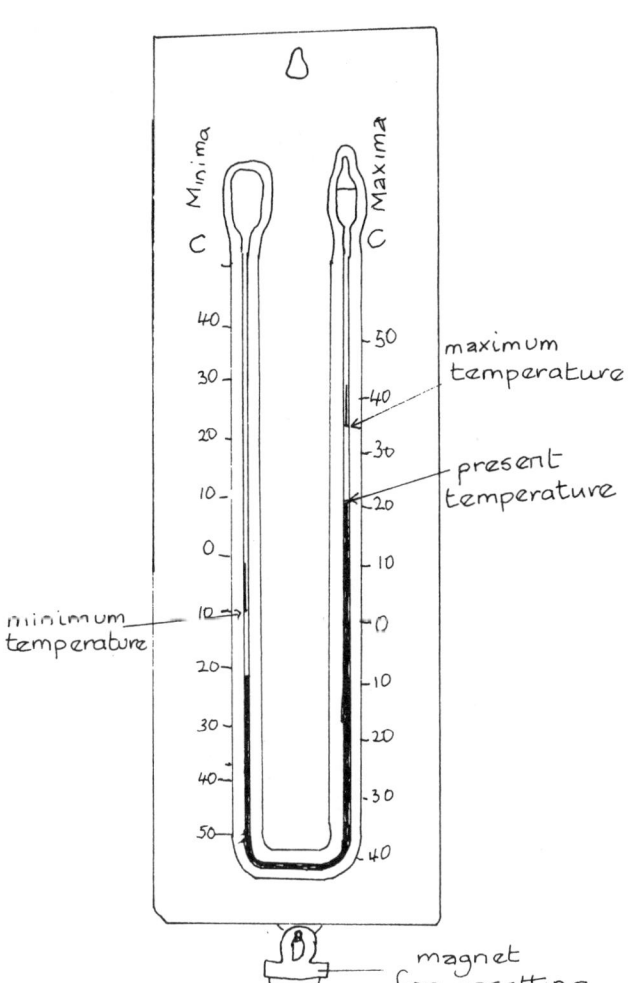

5a

Assignment Number 6

Recording Cloud Cover

P & C As part of the weather project (Assignment Numbers 1-5 and 7-9), you can keep records of cloud cover, using the accepted system below.

You will need:
Notebook, pencil.

Do this
1. Draw a circle each day about 4cm in diameter.
2. Mark on it how much of the sky is covered with cloud. Use the following symbols for guidance:

 sky clear

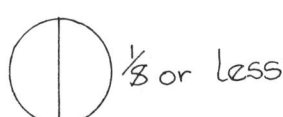 ⅛ or less

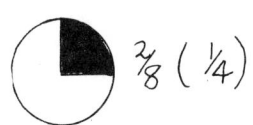 ²⁄₈ (¼)

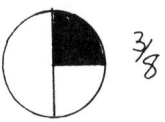 ³⁄₈

 ⁴⁄₈ (½)

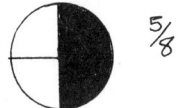 ⁵⁄₈

 ⁶⁄₈ (¾)

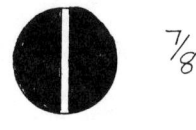 ⁷⁄₈

 overcast

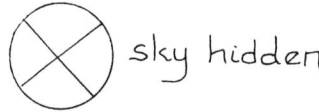 sky hidden

6a

Assignment Number 7

Rainfall Records

P & C Keeping details of rainfall is part of the weather project. Although expensive rainfall measuring equipment (the rain gauge) can be bought, you can make a simple one from easily obtainable plastic containers. It might even be possible to discover 'flaws' in your system.

You will need:
Notebook, pencil, large square plastic container (such as used for ice cream/margarine), small see-through plastic bottle, one larger plastic bottle of the same shape (we suggest large and small squash or fizzy drink bottles, but they must have flat bottoms, which are not shaped), ruler, sticky paper.

Do this
1 Cut the top off both the small and large polythene bottles.

2 You will need to compare the amounts of rainfall each day, so you will need to mark your container.

3 Cut out a strip of paper 10cm long.

4 Divide this into centimetres, and then each centimetre into millimetres.

5 Stick this onto the side of the smaller container.

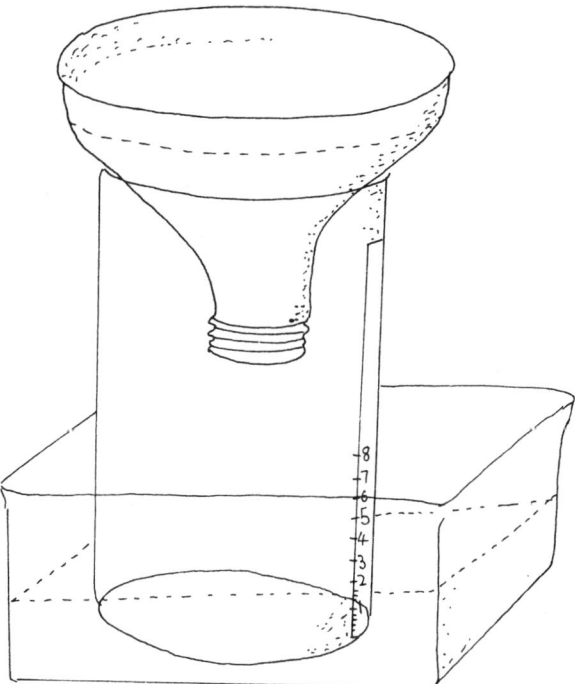

6 Use the top of the larger container to make a funnel.

7 Position your rain gauge in an open space.

8 Put it in a hole in the ground to stop it from blowing over. If this is not possible, arrange it in the plastic container with soil/sand to stabilise it.

9 Check your rainfall each day.

10 Record the amount by counting the marks. Keep your information on your record sheets, and on your weather board.

Think about this
1 Look at your cloud cover and rainfall records.

2 On very cloudy days did it always rain?

3 Can you discover what sort of clouds bring rain?

4 Try to find out why some areas have more rain than others.

5 If you have weather records for past years you could compare them.

Find out more
1 Weather at the Poles is different from that at the Equator. Can you discover something about why this is? Can you find out which place has the most rainfall?

2 Can you find out where (a) the wettest place in the world is (b) the driest place in the world is?

3 How do some plants manage to survive when there is no rain?

Assignment Number 8

Rain and Evaporation

P & C We have rain because of the phenomenon known as evaporation. There is water vapour in the atmosphere and when this condenses it forms droplets — the raindrops.

You cannot see evaporation taking place, because it is invisible. There are obvious times when it has taken place. For example, when a puddle dries up after a storm. We also see it when a car dries after it has been through a rainstorm. Clothes put out dry because the heat from the sun evaporates the water.

The rate at which evaporation takes place depends on the temperature. You will know, for example, that although clothes dry on a still cloudy day, it takes much longer than on a hot one.

You can investigate how temperature affects evaporation.

You will need:
Six equal sized small containers (round margarine tubs are suitable), three of which should have lids, measuring jug (or cylinder), felt tip pens which will mark on plastic, cold water, notebook, pencil, ruler.

Do this
1 Use the ruler to draw arrows at the same point on the inside of each container (see illustration).

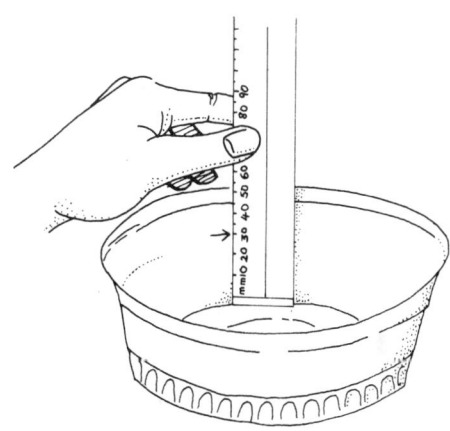

2 Number your containers 1 to 6.

3 Put water in all six containers so that it comes up to the arrows already made. This needs to be done carefully, to ensure that you get an accurate result.

4 Cover three with lids. These are the controls.

5 Put the containers in the following places:

  i In a warm place (no lid)
  ii In a warm place (with lid)
  iii In a cool place (no lid)
  iv In a cool place (with lid) (perhaps in a fridge if generally warm),
  v In a shaded place (no lid)
  vi In a shaded place (with lid) (cool cupboard, for example).

6 Have a record sheet in your notebook similar to the one below:

EVAPORATION

Date   Containers   1   2   3   4   5   6

7 Carefully investigate the containers each day for a week.

8 Measure the water in each container using the ruler.

9 Record the details in the chart.

10 Did you notice any difference between covered and uncovered containers?

11 Where was the container which lost (a) the most water (b) the least amount?

Think about this
1 Can you think of any reasons to explain what happened?

Primary 5 and 6
Evaporation goes on all the time. Discuss ways in which you can discover means of (a) speeding up the rate of evaporation and (b) slowing down the rate of evaporation.

You will need:
Kettle, stove, water, measuring jug, cold plate, notebook, pencil.

Do this
1 Put a measured amount of water in the kettle.
2 Note down how much it was in your notebook.
3 Place it on the stove to boil.
4 Watch what happens once the kettle boils.
5 Write down observations in activities notebook.

8a

Assignment Number 8

6 Hold a cold plate in front of the kettle spout — **take care.**
Do not get your fingers/hand near the spout.

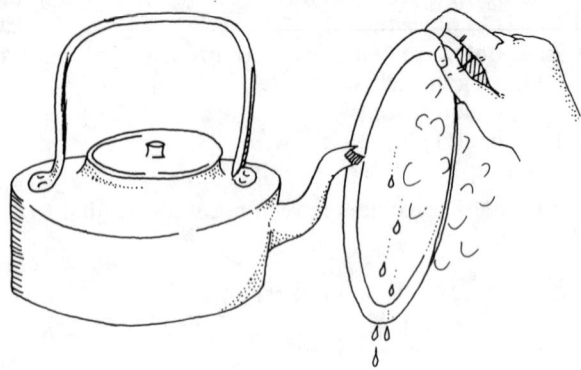

7 Observe and note what happens.

8 Leave the kettle to boil for 4-5 minutes.

9 Let the kettle cool down. Now pour the water back into the measuring jug.

10 How much water is there?

Think about this
1 Is there any change in the amount of water, before and after you heated it?

2 How have we speeded up evaporation?

3 What happened when you held the cold plate in front of the kettle spout?

4 Can you explain this?

Can you think of ways of slowing down the rate of evaporation? If you can, set up your own experiment.

Assignment Number 9

Making and using a Weather Vane

P & C In days gone by local people relied on various signs around them to give them an indication of what the weather was going to be like. They reinforced this with simple pieces of equipment, like the weather or wind vane. You can easily make your own. You could use this and your other weather equipment to compare your observations with modern weather forecasts.

Keeping weather records over a period of time will be useful in many ways. If careful records are kept you will be able to compare one year with another. In some instances, it is possible to see how weather patterns affect plant and animal growth.

You will need:
2m pole, 2 pieces of wood each about 60cm long, headless nail (or cut down knitting needle), drill, length of cane, piece of plastic from an ice cream or margarine container, ballpen cap, knife, directional compass.

Do this

1 Put the 2m pole in the ground, ensuring that it is firmly fixed.

2 Make slits in each end of the cane.

3 In one end put a square piece of plastic cut from the ice cream or margarine container.

4 In the other end put a small plastic arrow.

5 Make a hole in the cane to take the ball pen cap.

6 Knock the headless nail into the post.

7 Drill holes in the centre of the 60cm lengths of wood and attach these to the post, so that they face north, south, east and west.

8 Mark these directions on the wood. Make sure that you get them in the right place — check with your compass.

9 Gently drop the ball pen cap onto the nail.

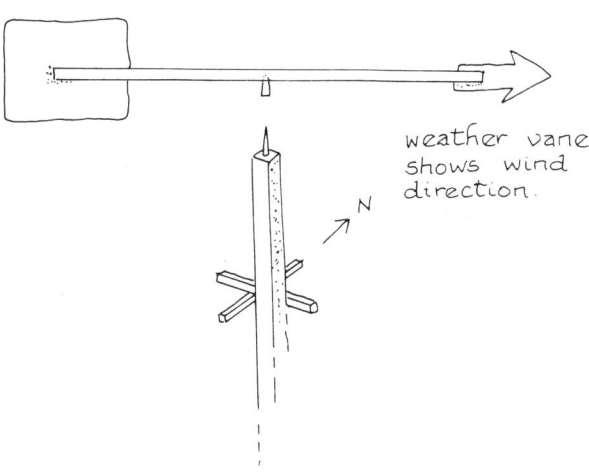

weather vane shows wind direction.

10 Make sure that it spins freely.

11 Use a wind rose to record your wind direction daily for each month.

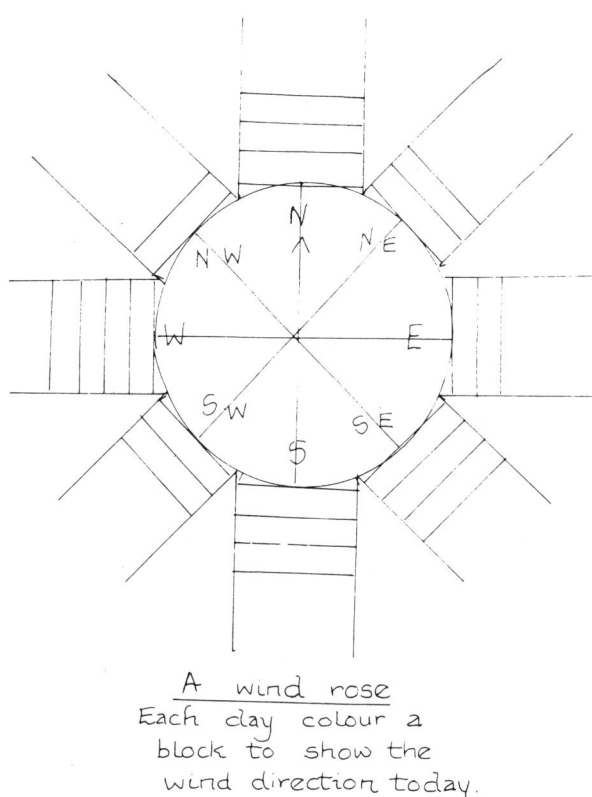

A wind rose
Each day colour a block to show the wind direction today.

Primary 5 and 6
Think about this

1 From the information which you collect, see if you can discover where the prevailing wind comes from each month.

2 Discover which winds bring different types of weather, such as rain.

3 By keeping records over a twelve month period, you will be able to see whether your observations about the direction which brings rain are consistent.

Assignment Number 9

Measuring Wind Speed

P & C When we listen to the radio, we are often told about gale force winds. This is especially true when we listen to the shipping forecast. If you can listen to a shipping forecast and a local weather forecast, see whether it is true that 'shipping forecasts issue gale warnings more often than land forecasts'.

You can make a simple piece of apparatus which will allow you to collect information about wind speeds. The piece of equipment is called an anemometer.

You will need:
Four yoghurt cartons, 2m pole, headless nail (or cut down knitting needle), 2 pieces of wood each 60cm long, nails, ballpen cap, notebook, pencil, drill, bright paint.

Do this
1 Drill a hole in the top of the post to take the headless nail (or the knitting needle).

2 Attach yoghurt cartons to the ends of the 60cm sticks. Make sure they are all facing in the same direction, otherwise they will not spin freely.

3 Drill a hole in the centre of the two sticks to take the ball pen cap.

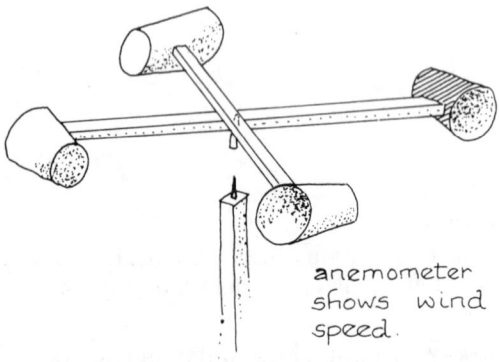

anemometer shows wind speed.

4 Gently lower the sticks onto the nail. Note that the ball pen cap should fit tightly into the hole in the stick to prevent these moving.

5 Paint one of the yoghurt cups a bright colour.

6 Although you will not get very accurate results from your home-made anemometer, at least it will give you enough information to be able to compare various days.

7 Keep your eye on the coloured yoghurt cup. Count how many times it goes round in a minute.

8 Do this every day. If you can do it at the same time each day, it is useful to compare your results.

9 Do not forget to keep a careful record of your results.

Primary 5 and 6
Think about this
1 Compare your results with radio forecasts.

2 Look at your wind vane directions. Try and link the two and see whether there is any connection between speed of wind and direction. For example, does the wind blow more strongly from the north? Does it blow more strongly and more often from one particular direction? Does it blow gently from some directions? Were there some days when you were not able to record the wind speed, because it was so calm?

3 Look at your daily weather temperature records. Can you compare wind direction, speed and temperatures? Do some winds bring warm weather, rain, cold weather, and so on?

Assignment Number 10

Finding Out About Shadows & Making A Shadow Clock

P Children are frequently aware of shadows. Sometimes they see their own shadows when they are out walking. Sometimes they do not see any at all. At other times they may stand in the shadow of a tree to keep cool.

Shadows can be investigated, without the need for sophisticated equipment. These simple investigations will give children some idea of shadow movements and they can make a shadow clock from their observations.

C Have you ever noticed how shadows change position as the day goes by? Have you ever noticed whether there are any changes in where shadows can be seen from day to day? You probably have noticed some of these things, but do you know how shadows change?

Using a tall stick, and taking measurements at regular intervals — in this case 30 minutes — you will be able to discover something about shadows. At the same time you will be able to make a shadow clock. You will be able to discover whether it is very accurate for telling the time.

You will need:
Notebook, pencil, long stick, timer/watch.

Do this

1 Put the stick in the ground on a sunny day. Make sure that it is not in the 'shadow' of buildings.

2 Make a chart in your notebook, so that you can record what you find out.

TIME	LENGTH OF SHADOW

3 Measure the length of the shadow every 30 minutes. Put your measurement in the table in your notebook.

Think about this

1 Was the length of the shadow always the same?

2 Did it get longer at any time?

3 Did it get shorter at any time?

4 Did you notice whether the shadows got shorter and then longer again?

5 If you found this, can you discover when it happened?

6 See if you can use your stick and shadows to tell the time.

7 You could try your experiment on (a) different days and (b) at different times of the year.

8 See whether you get the same readings (a) on different days and (b) at different times of the year.

9 You might be able to draw your results on graph paper. Draw your stick in the middle, and then draw the lengths of the shadows around this.

Primary 5 and 6
Find out more

See if you can find out anything else about shadows.

Find out how to make shadow puppets.

Compare your shadow with the shadows which you got from your face outlines. (See Assignment Number 77.)

See what you can find out about eclipses.

See what you can discover about clocks in history.

You might try making various other clocks for telling the time.

10 a

Assignment Number 11

Looking at Leaf Litter

P & C Animals have adapted to all sorts of habitats.
Walking over leaf litter — the debris which collects on the ground under trees, bushes and hedges — we usually think of it as being 'dead'. However, if we think about it, it soon becomes apparent that the leaf litter rots away, and in most areas breaks down. This is due to an extremely large number of animals — small creatures — which live there. We can investigate this. We can find out something about the creatures which live there, in the process, and try to discover what they do, how they move and so on.

You will need:
Pencil, notebook, piece of perforated zinc, (or perforated material, e.g. bandage), funnel, lamp, glass container, trowel (or similar tool for collecting leaf litter), a piece of white sheet or polythene (about 1 square metre), hand lens on string, polythene bags, small pots for taking specimens back, larger container such as a squash bottle cut down, table/anglepoise lamp, piece of card, sellotape.

Do this

1 You can carry out this study at various times of the year to discover whether there are any changes in the creatures which live in leaf litter.

2 Spread out your sheet or polythene on the ground.

3 Put a small amount of leaf litter on the sheet.

4 Spread this out.

5 Make sure your hand lens is round your neck, so that you do not lose it. Now look through your leaf litter. Push it to one side once you have sorted it.

6 Make a list of any animals which you find.

7 You will probably have difficulty naming many of them. Put them in small containers, so that you can identify them when you get back.

8 When you think you have discovered all the animals, put the leaf litter in a polythene bag to take back home with you.

9 When you get back you can set up a simple tullgren funnel. All you need is a container and a funnel. You can make the funnel out of the card. The illustration shows you how to set this up.

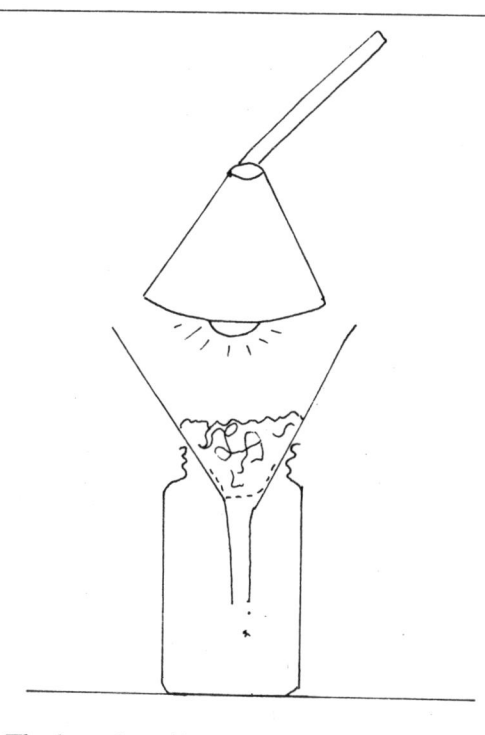

10 The heat from the lamp warms up the leaf litter. The animals living there do not like the warmth. Many of them would die if they dried up. They move away from the heat/light and drop into the container.

11 Keep a careful look out for animals which fall into the container.

12 Make sure that you do not let them die.

13 Identify the animals which you brought back.

14 If you can draw some of your animals, you could make a mobile from these, hanging them from cotton and pieces of twigs.

Primary 5 and 6
Do this

1 Find out which groups of animals your creatures belong to.

2 Try to identify as many as possible.

3 Discover how they move.

4 Try and find out what value they are in the litter.

5 See if you can find out what animals are eaten by other animals.

Assignment Number 12

Starting a Collection

P By instinct we are all collectors (some people would call some of us hoarders as well!). Early man was a collector. He collected the things around him which he needed for food. Children are natural collectors. They will collect from nature, as well as other things which interest them. From an early age this instinct to collect is noticeable. We can capitalise on it in some of our work.

C Have you ever collected anything? You must have at some time. We all collect. I used to collect colourful sweet wrappers when I was a little boy. You might collect photographs of pop stars, or footballers. When you are outside you might even collect natural things. We are going to make collections and then use these when looking at some of our other Assignment sheets. We will be able to sort things out, to see which are alike (Assignment sheet 29).

You will need:
Paper or card for mounting, feathers, piece of hardboard (this should be just a bit bigger than the paper or card which you are using), pencil, ruler, notebook, sharp cutting blade — knife, razor blade, etc., BUT be careful, ask an adult to help you, PDB or naphthalene, plastic bags.

Do this
1 Collect feathers, which you will find in all sorts of places. You will probably find a lot on your walks. If you live in a town, you will probably also find a lot there.

2 When you collect your feathers, put them in plastic bags.

3 You could put in naphthalene — the stuff which moth balls are made of, or some PDB (this is paradichlor-benzine). This will get rid of any small creatures — called mites — which are in the feathers. Sometimes the moth which attacks clothes will also attack the feathers. Putting the feathers in one or other of these substances stops this happening.

4 Sometimes you might find a dead bird. You can take feathers from this. It is better to use rubber gloves while doing this, as birds sometimes carry diseases. ALWAYS wash your hands after touching feathers or dead birds.

5 You can make an attractive collection of your feathers.

6 Use the plain sheet of paper, and arrange various feathers which you have collected. Try various arrangements until you are happy with one that suits you.

7 You will have to take your feathers off before you can mount them properly.
Before you do this, draw round the outline very faintly with pencil.

8 Take off the feathers and make som careful slits in the paper. These slits will take your feathers.

9 If you have a long feather, you will probably need two slits: a small feather will only require one.

10 If you know which birds the feathers came from, add this information. If you do not, try to find out.

Think about this
1 Look at your different feathers, and try to discover how they are different.

2 Try to find out where the different feathers come from — for example, which part of the birds do the soft, downy feathers come from?

Find out more
1 Try to find out as much as you can about feathers and flight.

12 a

Assignment Number 13

Making Simple Keys

P There are various ways of identifying plants and animals. One of the simplest, and one which younger children will employ is to match what they have against a picture, which might be a photograph or a drawing. There comes a point, however, when closely related species cannot be separated in this way, and we have to resort to more sophisticated methods. These involve the use of keys. The keys give us a choice of important features about a plant or an animal. By following these we should be able to identify our specimen.

Keys are generally quite complicated, but children can make their own simple ones. One of the reasons for doing this is that it teaches children to observe very carefully.

The first key can be made using six very simple different objects from around the house. This can be followed up by one using common plants.

C When we start to find out what things are, we match what we have with pictures and drawings. Sometimes, however, there comes a point when this is no longer possible. This happens when we have found two things which look almost identical — to some of us they might even look identical. We then have to use keys. Just as a door key unlocks doors, so a plant or animal key unlocks the 'mystery' and lets us discover what the plant or animal is.

You will need:
Collect six objects from around the house. If possible try and select six objects which you do not know the names of, and which are different in colour, feel, size and so on, notebook, pencil, ruler.

Do this

1 Make a recording sheet in your notebook, like the one below.

Table 1 Making a key, stage one

Description	object number					
	1	2	3	4	5	6

2 You will need to look carefully at each of the six objects in turn.

3 Select the first object. Write down **one** word at a time to describe it. You write these words in the wide column and put a tick in the second (first narrow) column.

4 Write down any other words which you think might also describe the first object. Put the describing words in the first column and add the ticks in the first narrow column. Table 2 shows this.

Table 2 Making a key, stage two

Description	object number					
	1	2	3	4	5	6
Glass	✓					
With tip	✓					
Round	✓					

5 Now choose your second object. If anything you have used to describe the first object can also be used for the second one, just place a tick in the second (narrow) column. See Table 3.

Table 3 Making a key, stage three

Description	object number					
	1	2	3	4	5	6
Glass	✓					
With tip	✓					
Round	✓					
Brown		✓				
Card		✓				
With flaps		✓				

13 a

6 Work through each of the objects, and you will have a chart similar to Table 4 — but with your own words on it!

Table 4 Making a key, stage four

KEY MAKING SHEET						
Description	\multicolumn{6}{c}{object number}
	1	2	3	4	5	6
Glass	✓				✓	
With tip	✓				✓	
Round	✓					
Brown		✓				✓
Card		✓				
With flaps		✓				
Green			✓			
Metal			✓			
Black					✓	
Rubber					✓	
Hexagonal					✓	
Cylinder						✓
Rough						
Clear		✓				
Oblong			✓			

7 Look carefully at the lists. Look at Table 4 first, and then at your own. You will see that some words are used to describe a number of objects in our Table 4. Others have only been used to describe one object.

8 Put a line through any of yours which have been used to describe more than one object. We have done this for our list. You will see it if you look at Table 5.

Table 5 Making a key, stage five

KEY MAKING SHEET						
Description	\multicolumn{6}{c}{object number}
	1	2	3	4	5	6
~~Glass~~	✓				✓	
~~With tip~~	✓				✓	
Round	✓					
~~Brown~~		✓				✓
Card		✓				
With flaps		✓				
Green			✓			
Metal			✓			
Black					✓	
Rubber					✓	
Hexagonal					✓	
Cylinder						✓
Rough						✓
Clear		✓				
Oblong			✓			

There is at least one word for each object. This word is not used for any of the others. Using these words we can make a simple key, so that we could identify these **same** six objects if they were placed in front of us again.

We have made a simple key using the words in Table 5.

Simple key made from Table 5

1. Clear
   Not clear 2
2. Oblong
   Not oblong 3
3. Green
   Not green 4
4. Black
   Not black 5
5. Cylinder
   Not cylinder 6
6. Rough

9 Use your words to work out a similar key for your own objects. You can add the names of the objects now. If you do not know them you will be able to find out.

10 When you want to use the key for identifying objects you will see that there are two alternatives. Either what you are looking at fits the descriptive word, or it does not. If it does not, then you move on to the next word (2).

If you look at our example, you will see that for object (1), the two alternatives which we have are 'clear' and 'not clear'. The clear object is the beaker. If the object which we have in front of us is 'not clear', then it is not the beaker, and we move on to (2).

We will be able to identify all our objects eventually. But of course we can only identify the objects which appear in the key.

11 Give your key to someone else to use, and they should be able to tell you whether it works or not. If they can use it, it is a good key. If they cannot, it is not much good.

12 Now collect six different flowers from your garden. Make a key using these.

Assignment Number 14

Looking at Soil

P Soil is often taken for granted. Yet it is important because it is the 'substance' in which plants grow. Plants are the only living things which can use the energy from the sun to make their food. All animals are dependent on the plants, which grow in the soil.

Soil makes a fascinating study, and there are many investigations which can be carried out. The purpose of these studies is to show children that the soil is living, and that many fascinating things go on in it.

C Soil is very important to us. We grow our crops in it. How much do you know about it? In these investigations we will be able to discover many things. This will help us to build up a better picture of the soil.

You will need:
Spade, trowel, containers for carrying soil in, labels, notebook, pencil, white tray, hand lens, microscope, nature viewer, jars, water, soil samples from different places, newspaper, plain white paper.

Primary 3 and 4
A look at soil
1 Spread some soil onto white paper or a piece of newspaper.

2 Sort through this.

3 Use your hand lens to look more closely at the soil.

4 Make a list of all the things which you find in your soil.

5 If you find any very small creatures in your soil, put them in small containers, so that you can look at them further.

6 Look at any small creatures which you have found. Put them in a nature viewer, under the microscope or view them with a hand lens.

7 When you have finished looking at them, release them. Put them in the soil in your garden.

See if you can answer some of these questions about your soil.

8 Feel your soil. What does it feel like?

9 Rub it between your fingers. Does it leave a stain? Does it stick?

10 Was the soil wet or dry?

11 Was it lumpy?

12 Did you find any roots in it?

13 What sort of animals — if any — did you find in it?

Primary 5 and 6
Soil profile
Soil changes as we move further from the surface. The most fertile area, where most plants grow, is in the top layer.

1 Use your spade to dig a hole. Do it carefully, and you will see the soil profile — the layers.

2 Each soil profile will be different. They often vary quite a lot within a short distance.

3 We show you a profile, as an example.

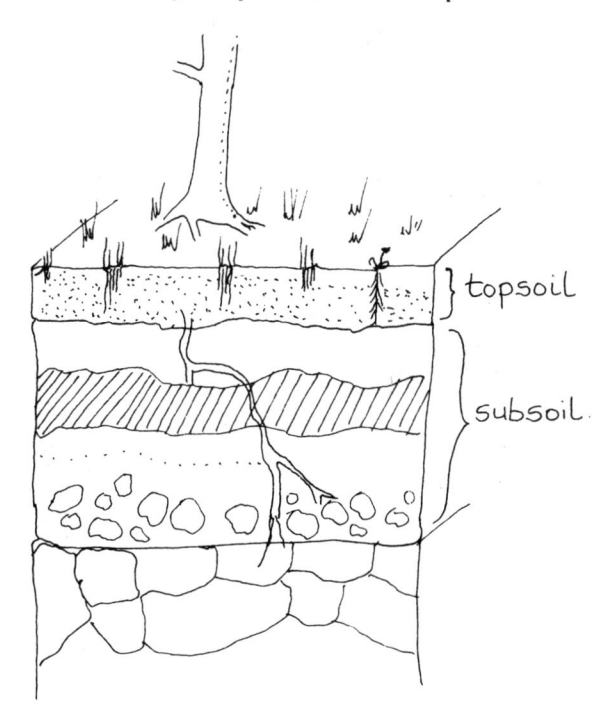

4 Look at your profile and then draw it. You could use coloured pencils to show the different coloured layers.

5 Put some of the soil in polythene bags, and take it back with you for further study.

What is the soil made up of?
Look at each of the different soils which you have collected. See if you can discover what it is that makes them different.

Primary 5 and 6
Chemical analysis of the soil
When we looked through our soil samples, we found various things. There were probably pieces of roots, stones, etc. You can sort out some of the things in the soil by following these instructions.

14 a

Assignment Number 14

Do this
1 Put about 5cm of soil in the bottom of a jar.

2 Do this with different soil samples. Make sure that there is about the same amount of soil in each jar. If you do this, you will be able to compare your soils more easily.

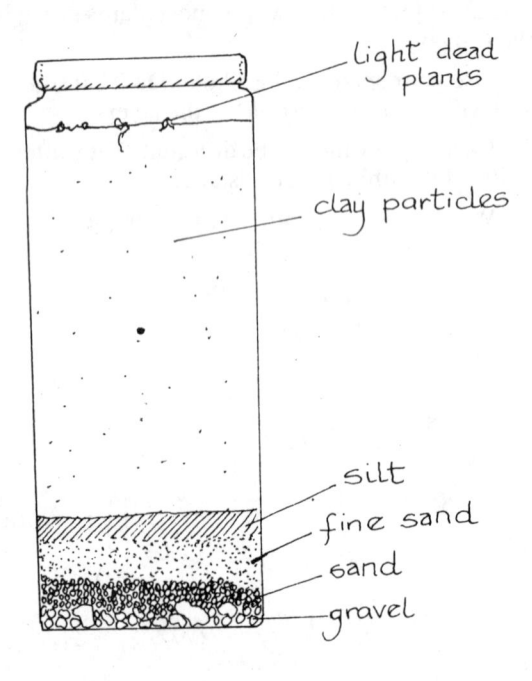

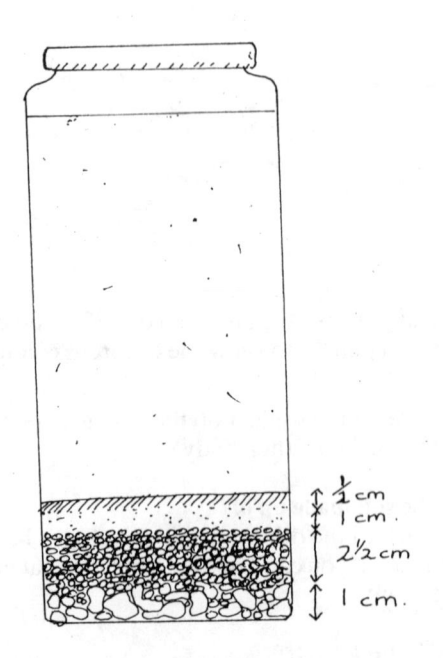

[Diagram of jar labelled: light dead plants, clay particles, silt, fine sand, sand, gravel]

[Diagram of jar with measurements: ½ cm, 1 cm, 2½ cm, 1 cm]

3 Fill each jar nearly to the top with water.

4 Put a lid on the jar tightly!

5 Shake up each of the jars. Make sure that the soil and water are thoroughly mixed.

6 Allow them to settle.

Think about this
1 Can you see different layers in your jars?

2 Draw each jar side by side, so that you can show the various layers, and compare them.

3 If you look carefully at your jars you will see that the heaviest things have sunk to the bottom, and the lightest material is floating on the top.

4 If the water stays cloudy, this is probably because the very smallest particles — called clay — are floating around in the water. You will probably find that they eventually settle.

5 Compare the layers in your various jars to see what differences there are.

6 Measure each of the layers with your ruler.

7 If you measure the distance as shown in the diagram, you can work out the percentage which each layer takes up.

Different soil types
There are different soil types. You can discover which kind yours is by using a simple key. The key is set out on p14c. and to work it out you start where it says 'Start here'.

1	Is it gritty?	Yes	Sandy Soil
		No	See (2)
2	Does it feel silky?	Yes	Loam
		No	See (3)
3	Is it sticky?	Yes	Clay soil

and so on. If you have made a mistake the key will take you back to the beginning.

Primary 5 and 6
Micro-organisms in the soil
There are many very small organisms in the soil. They are so small that we cannot see them with the naked eye. We call these micro-organisms. The word 'micro' tells us that they are very small. Amongst these are fungi and bacteria. It is possible to grow them on culture plates, where you can see them more easily. NB Some of them could be harmful, so take great care and follow the instructions.

You will need:
Notebook, pencil, small round petri dishes (you could use jar lids and clingfilm instead) soil, needle, sellotape, labels, light coloured table jelly, Oxo, match (ask an adult for help).

Do this
1 Dissolve a small amount of the jelly and add a small amount of Oxo, Bovril or similar material to it. This will provide food.

2 Pour jelly into two petri dishes or two lids. (If using plastic lids wait until the jelly cools down.)

3 Take a small amount of the soil on the end of the needle, and scrape it across the surface of the jelly when it has set in **one** of the dishes.

Assignment Number 14

4 Do not do anything to the jelly in the other dish. This is the control.

5 Cover both dishes. Seal with sellotape. If using dish lids instead of dishes, cover with clingfilm and seal with sellotape.

6 Label the dishes: include the date, which dish has been treated: which is the control.

7 Place both dishes in a warm place.

8 Look at your dishes regularly and record what you see.

9 Do not take off the lids.

10 If anything happens to the jelly which has been treated with the soil, this will give you an idea of some of the micro-organisms which live in the soil.

11 Repeat this with various soils.

12 Try and compare your results.

13 Wrap your dishes in polythene bags and put in the dustbin.

Think about this

1 Can you think of any value which these micro-organisms might have in the soil?

2 Try and discover as much as you can about useful and harmful micro-organisms — not just in the soil.

3 Can you think of any micro-organisms which might affect you? What might they do?

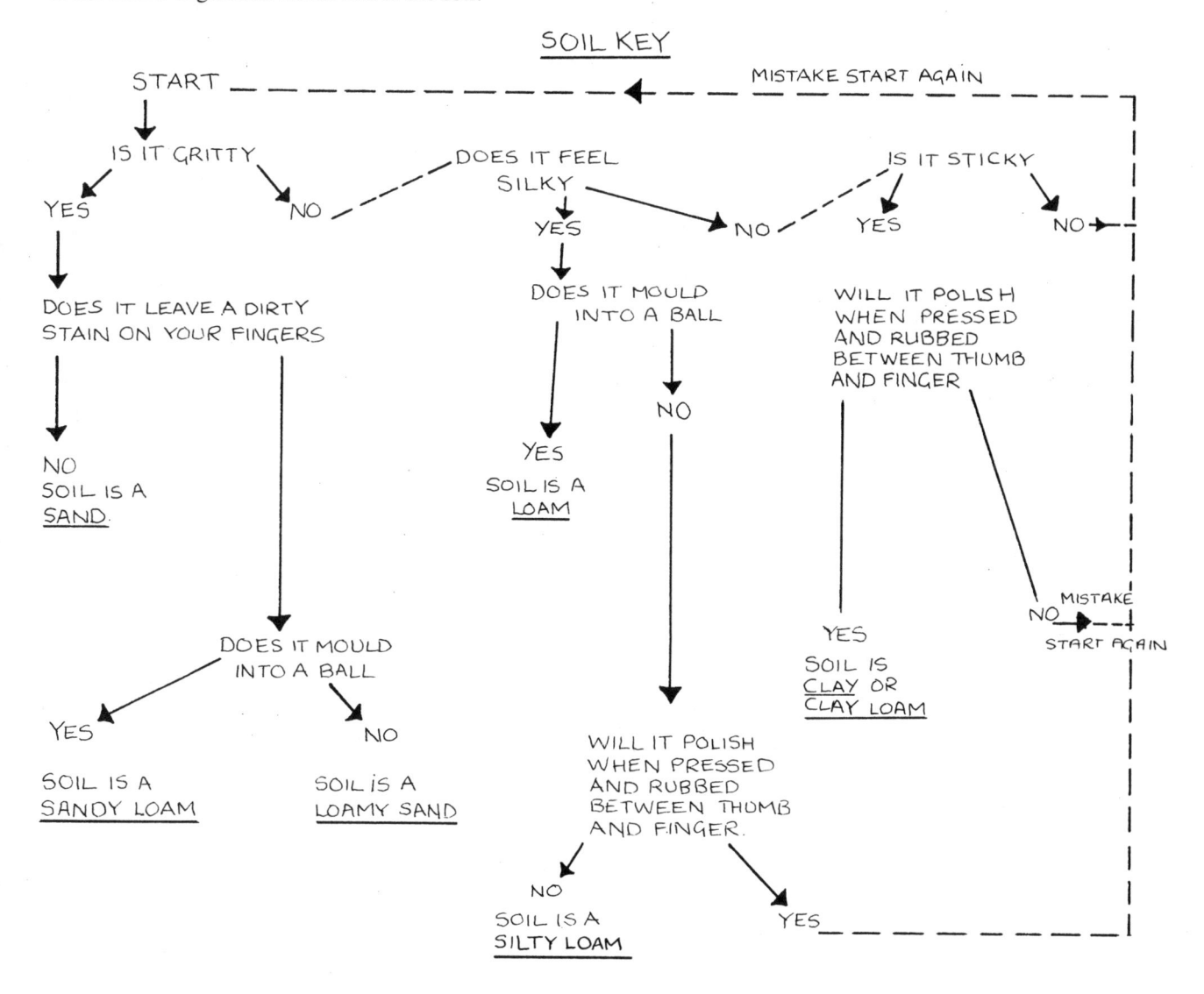

SOIL KEY

START → IS IT GRITTY
- YES → DOES IT LEAVE A DIRTY STAIN ON YOUR FINGERS
  - NO → SOIL IS A SAND.
  - (YES) → DOES IT MOULD INTO A BALL
    - YES → SOIL IS A SANDY LOAM
    - NO → SOIL IS A LOAMY SAND
- NO → DOES IT FEEL SILKY
  - YES → DOES IT MOULD INTO A BALL
    - YES → SOIL IS A LOAM
    - NO → WILL IT POLISH WHEN PRESSED AND RUBBED BETWEEN THUMB AND FINGER
      - NO → SOIL IS A SILTY LOAM
      - YES → (back to start)
  - NO → IS IT STICKY
    - YES → WILL IT POLISH WHEN PRESSED AND RUBBED BETWEEN THUMB AND FINGER
      - YES → SOIL IS CLAY OR CLAY LOAM
      - NO → MISTAKE START AGAIN
    - NO → MISTAKE START AGAIN

FROM 'A FIELD APPROACH TO BIOLOGY' © R.Wilson and D.Wright.

Assignment Number 15

Bird Feeding Project

P We often think that we know a great deal about the animals which we consider a part of our everyday lives. Birds are no exception. We see them when we are out, and we watch them when they come into the garden. But how much do we know about their feeding habits? This project will give us some information.

C If you were asked to make a list of the different kinds of food eaten by the birds which you see you probably would not get very far. How much do you know about what birds eat? Do you know whether some species like one kind of food and not another? In our bird feeding project we can find out.

Primary 3 and 4
You will need:
Bird table and various kinds of food, pair of binoculars, notebook, pencil.

Do this
1 If you do not have a bird table, or cannot buy one, you can probably get one made.

2 Make a tray from a square piece of wood, and add four pieces of wood for the sides to prevent food from falling off.

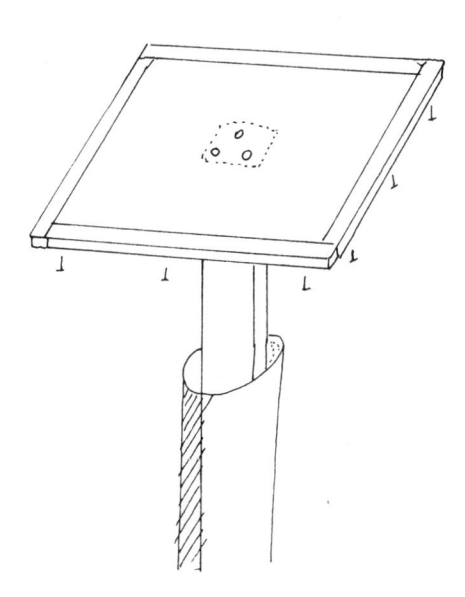

3 Mount it on a wooden post.

4 If you can make a roof for your bird table, so much the better.

5 You can place your bird table in the garden.

6 If you want to move the table about, you will need to nail some pieces of wood onto the post to form a stand. Make sure that it is stable, otherwise it will probably blow over in high winds.

7 If you are troubled by cats climbing onto the table, you need to take various precautions. Ensure that the table is not close to any objects which the cats can use as 'jumping' or 'launching' pads. Cover the post with a piece of plastic drainpipe. This prevents cats from climbing up and getting on to the table.

8 If you do not want to have a fixed bird table, or cannot find a suitable post, you can always add some chains, or wire, and hang the bird table from a tree or from an outhouse. Again, however, you need to beware of intruders, like cats, squirrels, etc.

9 Provide a wide variety of food for your birds. You will probably find that you get many birds coming to your bird table. Some of these will eat insects, some seeds, and some a mixture. Some birds feed on the ground. Provide food for these too.

10 Keep a chart in your notebook to record what you observe.

Date	Name of bird	Food eaten

Think about this
1 Look at your lists. Do you think that there are some sorts of birds which do not come to the garden?

2 Was there any kind of food which was not eaten by some birds?

3 Were there other species which were less fussy?

4 Can you sort out your birds in to various groups depending on the sorts of food which they eat?

5 Do some birds have different sorts of beaks to deal with the various kinds of food?

Do this
1 Birds also need water. They use this for drinking and for bathing in.

2 You could provide your birds with water

3 You could provide this in an upturned dustbin lid. If you use this put a brick in it to prevent it from falling over. Put in a plant pot and add a branch or two so that the birds have somewhere to perch.

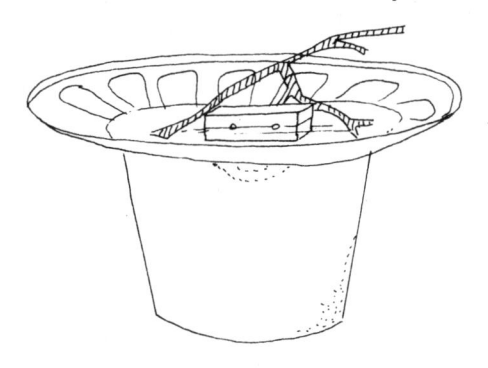

Sample setting of Nature Walk No. 15

Think about this
1 Having watched your birds, can you discover whether some come to drink and some to bathe?

Do this
1 In cold weather put out a biscuit tin upside down over a night light. Put your water container on top of the biscuit tin. This will provide enough heat to keep the water free from ice. An alternative method is to use bricks instead of a biscuit tin.

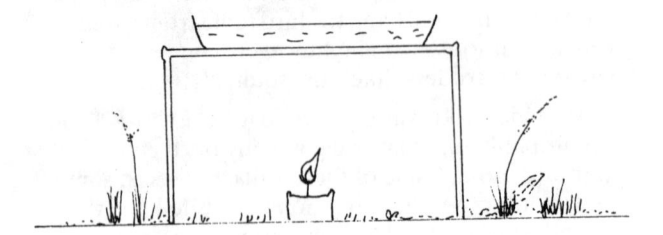

Find out more
1 Try to discover as many of the different sorts of birds as possible which live in your area.

2 See if you can find out what sort of beaks they have, and whether these are suitable for the jobs which they have to do.

3 See if you can find out where your birds (a) nest (b) feed and (c) roost.

4 See if you can discover what birds do at night.

Assignment Number 16

What Seeds do Birds Like?

P When we think of seed-eating birds, we think of them as eating seeds. We seldom know — or perhaps even think — whether birds have preferences for certain seeds. In the autumn, there are certain seeds in the garden and in the countryside which are eaten first. We can carry out a simple investigation to see which seeds are the most popular.

C You will probably know that some of the birds which come into your garden, or which you see in the countryside are seed-eaters. Have you ever wondered whether they eat any seeds in particular, or whether they are rather more fussy. We can have a look at this problem, by offering birds a variety of seeds to see what happens.

You will need:
A collection of various seeds (you could collect seeds while you are out on your walk through the summer and autumn. If you do, place them in polythene bags, and label them), piece of wood about 1 metre long by 15cm wide, several small 'dishes' — these could be jam jar lids, or other screw-top lids. If possible ensure that they are all the same sort and size, glue, post about 2m long, notebook, pencil, hammer, screw, nails.

Do this
1 Decide how many lids you can fix along the length of the wood. Attach them to the piece of wood with glue, or nail them on.

2 Hammer the post into the ground.

3 Screw the piece of wood to the post.

4 Put seeds into each of the 'dishes'. Make sure that each 'dish' only has one kind of seed in it.

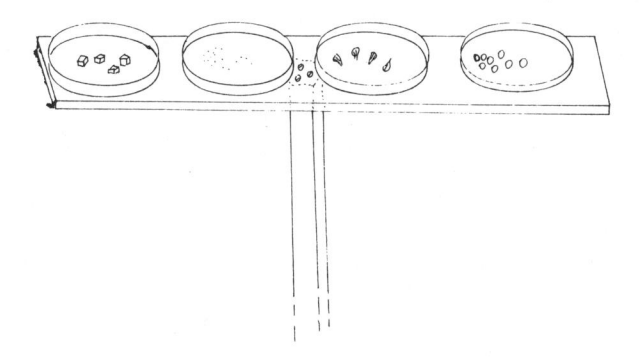

5 Keep a record of the birds which come, and the seeds which they eat.

6 If you repeat your investigation over several days, you will be able to see whether some seeds are more popular than others.

7 Do not forget to put different seeds in different cups.

Think about this
1 Did some birds prefer some seeds, and leave others?

2 Do you think the birds might have eaten all the seeds eventually?

You could repeat your investigation and try this. You could also leave the experiment, or even repeat it, when there is very cold weather. You can only do this investigation in certain places.

16a

Assignment Number 17

When do Birds come to Feed?

P Almost anywhere that we live, we have birds coming into the garden. Yet, it is fairly safe to suggest that few of us know much about when birds come to feed. This simple investigation, will not only teach children to be observant, but it will also provide valuable information about bird feeding habits.

C I should imagine that you have birds coming to your garden to feed. Do you have several different species? If you do, do you know what time they come? I should imagine you probably know very little. In this project we should be able to discover something about the times when various species visit the garden.

You will need:
Food for your birds, notebook, pencil.

Do this

1 We want to find out what time birds come, so we always need to have a supply of food on the bird table. Make sure that there is always plenty. There should be food early in the morning, and there should be food there at dusk. Ensure that you leave plenty of food out for at least a week before you start carrying out your studies. By doing this you will encourage the birds to visit you regularly.

2 In your notebook, make a list of the birds which are feeding on your bird table for fifteen minutes at the beginning of every hour for one day.

3 At the same time, keep a note about weather conditions. If you are working on your weather assignment, you will also be collecting this information.

4 Collect this information for one session each day for a week.

5 Try to collect the same information in different weather conditions.

6 Try to collect the same information at different seasons of the year.

Think about this

1 Did you notice whether some birds came at some times and not at others?

2 Do some birds come at various times throughout the day?

3 Do weather conditions affect whether birds come or whether they stay away?

4 Did you find that there were some weather conditions when no birds came?

5 Some birds do not like windy weather. Did you discover any of these?

17th May 1982.
20°C Wind 5.1 rev/min
Birds visiting our table:-

Time	
9.0–9.15	3 blackbirds, robin.
10.0–10.15	
11.0–11.15	
12.0–12.15	
1.0–1.15	
2.0–2.15	
3.0–3.15	
4.0–4.15	
5.0–5.15	
6.0–6.15	
7.0–7.15	
8.0–8.15	
9.0–9.15	
9.45	Sunsets.

Assignment Number 18

Bird Nesting Boxes

P & C We can sometimes encourage birds into our garden by putting up nest boxes. If we are able to do this, we are likely to learn a great deal about them.

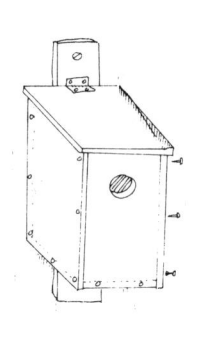

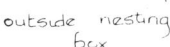

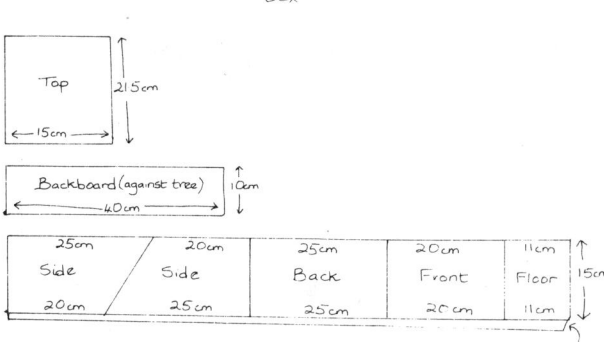

outside nesting box

Top 21·5cm, 15cm

Backboard (against tree) 10cm, 40cm

| 25cm Side 20cm | 20cm Side 25cm | 25cm Back 25cm | 20cm Front 20cm | 11cm Floor 11cm | 15cm |

18mm

One of the best ways of siting a nest box is on the inside of a shed or other wooden outbuilding. By drilling a hole into the wall of a shed you will give the bird an entrance into the nest box which is attached to the inside. You can see this in the section drawing. Other nest boxes can be attached to walls and trees (see diagram). The advantage of putting one on the inside of a building is that it is possible to fit a glass back, and a removeable plate. Careful observations can then be made at regular intervals.

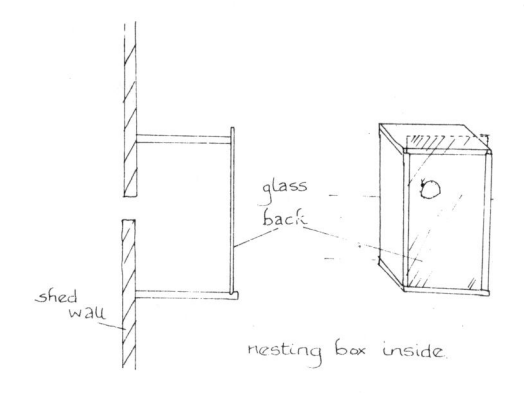

shed wall — glass back — nesting box inside

You will need:
Nest box, notebook, pencil, coloured wool.

Do this
1 Put your nest box up several months before nesting starts. This will help the birds to get used to it. Make sure that your nest box is fixed in a suitable position. If you cannot attach it as suggested above, you may be able to use a dining room, or other window. The nest box has to be attached to the outside of the window. Black paper has to cover the inside of the window. You will not be able to do this very satisfactorily if you choose a position in which your window heats up from the sun.

2 Put out coloured wool.

3 Keep an eye on the birds to see whether they come and take it. To attract various birds you could put some wool on the clothes line, and some on the ground.

4 Keep a careful check on your nest box to see whether any birds come into it.

Think about this
1 If a bird does not use your nest box, can you think of a reason?

2 You might find that you need to move it about from time to time — don't do it too often, as the birds need to get used to it.

3 Do birds use it outside the breeding season? If so, what for?

☐

18 a

Make a Pooter

P & C Pooters are useful for collecting small animals which it is not possible to pick up with the hands. They would escape. Once a pooter has been made, it can be used in a number of Assignments.

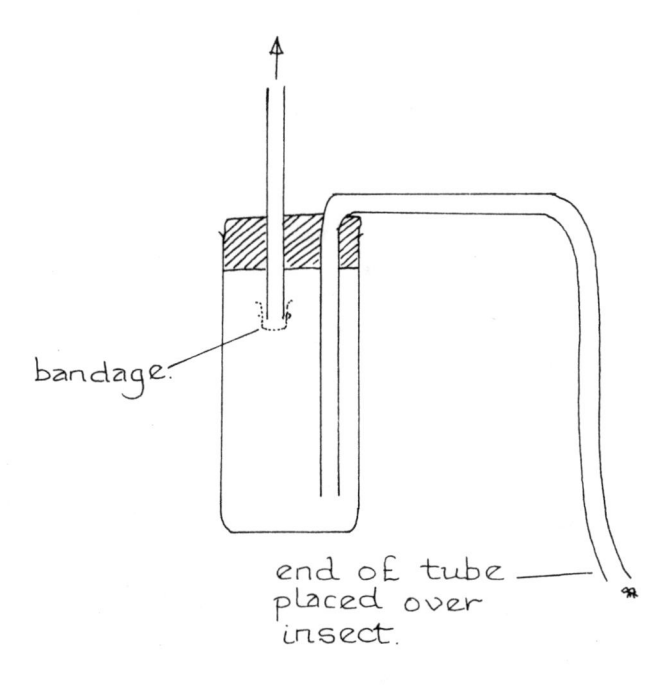

bandage

end of tube placed over insect.

You will need:
Small plastic (clear) bottle (or glass one, if a plastic one is not available), plastic tubing, cork, piece of nylon stocking (or bandage), cotton, nail or sharp knitting needle.

Do this
1 Make up the pooter as shown in the diagram.

2 The holes are bored into the cork with the knitting needle to take the two plastic tubes. These should fit tightly.

3 Cover the end of the shorter tube with a piece of nylon stocking or bandage.

4 When collecting insects you suck through the shorter tube, which is covered with the nylon or bandage.

5 If you have a number of pots and corks the same size, you can simply transfer the cork and tubes from one container to another, when you have caught some of the animals.

Assignment Number 20

Looking at and Keeping Minibeasts

P It has become fashionable to call small invertebrates — animals without backbones, like spiders, snails, centipedes, etc — minibeasts. During your various expeditions you will come across a wide variety of these. There is seldom time to study them in detail while you are out. You might notice one or two things about them — how quickly they move, how they feed, for example. Most minibeasts can easily be kept in simple containers. These animals provide a valuable source of material to study. We suggest one or two here, and offer a useful book in the booklist.

C You have probably noticed all kinds of small animals when you have been out on your travels, and your regular walk. Sometimes these are a nuisance, especially when they bite and sting. There are many of these invertebrates — animals without a backbone. We call them minibeasts. We can collect some, and keep them for a short time in captivity. In doing so we shall be able to study them much more closely than if they were in the wild state. You probably know how, when you are just about to look at a spider, for example, it scuttles off into the undergrowth.

KEEPING WORMS
You will need:
Jam jar, black paper or black polythene, cardboard, soil, sand, peat, chalk (but not blackboard chalk), worms, pieces of leaves/other food materials.

Do this
1 Make a tube from the card, so that it will stand in the middle of the jar. If you do not do this, you may find that the worms burrow into the material towards the centre of the jar, and you will not be able to see their activities.

2 Put in a layer of soil between the cardboard and the side of the jar.

3 Add to this a layer of peat.

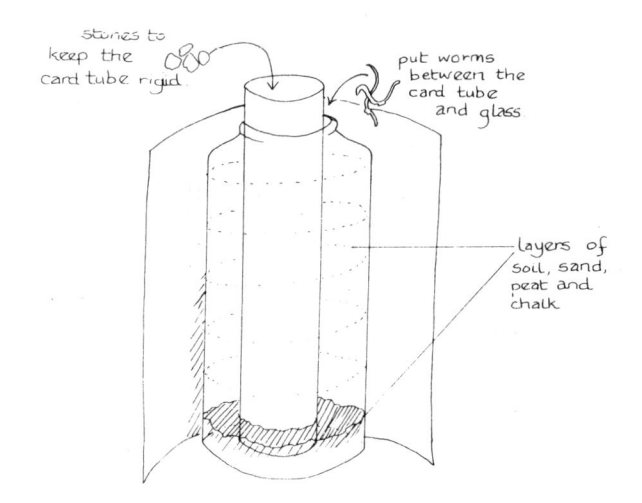

4 Continue adding alternate layers until the jar is almost full.

5 If you find that the cardboard in the centre starts to collapse under the weight of the soil which you are adding, fill the centre part with soil.

6 Make sure that the layers of soil, sand, etc which you have put in are always moist, otherwise the worms will die.

7 Now place some worms on the top of the soil, in the area between the cardboard and the sides of the glass.

8 Cover the outside of the jar with black paper or polythene. Can you think why you might have done this? If you think where the worms normally live, or where you collected them from, you should soon realise why you have done this.

9 Place various pieces of different leaves and other kinds of food — like carrot, for example — on top of the soil.

10 Take off the paper at regular intervals to see what is going on underneath.

11 Keep your eye on the soil surface to see whether anything has happened to the food which you put there.

Think about this
1 If your earthworms survive — and there is no reason why they should not — then you should be able to describe what happens inside the container.

Find out more
The famous scientist Charles Darwin did a lot of research about worms. He gave them a name which described their work. See if you can find out what he called them. If you compare what happened in your jar with what Darwin discovered you will soon be able to see why he gave them this name.

Assignment Number 21

Finding out about Insects

P Insects are around us all the time. Sometimes we fail to see what good some of them do. Flies, for example, fall into this category. But there are others like bees and butterflies which are useful. Wasps, although despised at certain seasons of the year, are useful for most of the time. Early in the year they take many grubs and pests in the garden. If these grubs were allowed to develop they would do a great deal of damage to the gardener's crops.

Careful records of insect activity will lead to a better understanding of them. As well as observing them in their natural environment we can also keep them for further study.

It is useful for children to get into the habit of ensuring that they record certain details. This consistency will lead them into making careful observations as they gain experience and confidence.

C Insects are all around us. By keeping these you will be able to find out more about them. Caterpillars are one of the most fascinating groups of insects to keep, since it is often possible to see changes which take place, as they change from caterpillar to adult.

You will need
Notebook, cotton wool, plastic container (use any transparent plastic container from which the bottom has been removed), pencil, paintbrush, muslin (or substitute), 12cm flower pot, soil, elastic band, small bottle.

Do this
1   Fill the plant pot with soil.
2   Push the smaller bottle into this.
3   Look for some caterpillars. When you have found some, you will need to find out what plants they feed on.
4   Collect some of the food and place it in the smaller bottle in some water. Plug the top with cotton wool to prevent any caterpillars from falling in and drowning.
5   Introduce your caterpillars on to the food plant.
6   Cover the smaller bottle with the larger one.
7   Put the muslin over the open end of this, and secure with an elastic band.

Daily routine
1   Each day check the food plant. Make sure there is a good supply.
2   Replace the food plant as necessary.
3   Take out the waste.
4   Keep a careful record of your observations.

Primary 5 and 6
Do this
1   Measure your caterpillars regularly.
2   Keep careful records.
3   At intervals caterpillars moult — shed their skins. Watch for this and note down what happens.
4   Take your caterpillars out carefully when you are looking for them.
5   Draw graphs to show how your caterpillars grow. If possible use a number of caterpillars so that you can compare their growth rates.

21a

Assignment Number 21

Think about this

1 You should be able to discover whether all caterpillars manage to change their skins at the same time.

2 You should be able to discover whether they all grow at the same rate.

3 The caterpillars of most butterflies will climb onto the muslin to pupate. Those of moths will go into the soil. Some butterflies might go down into the soil.

4 Keep careful observations of when this happens.

Primary 5 and 6
You might find other invertebrates. Use the key to help you discover to which group they belong.

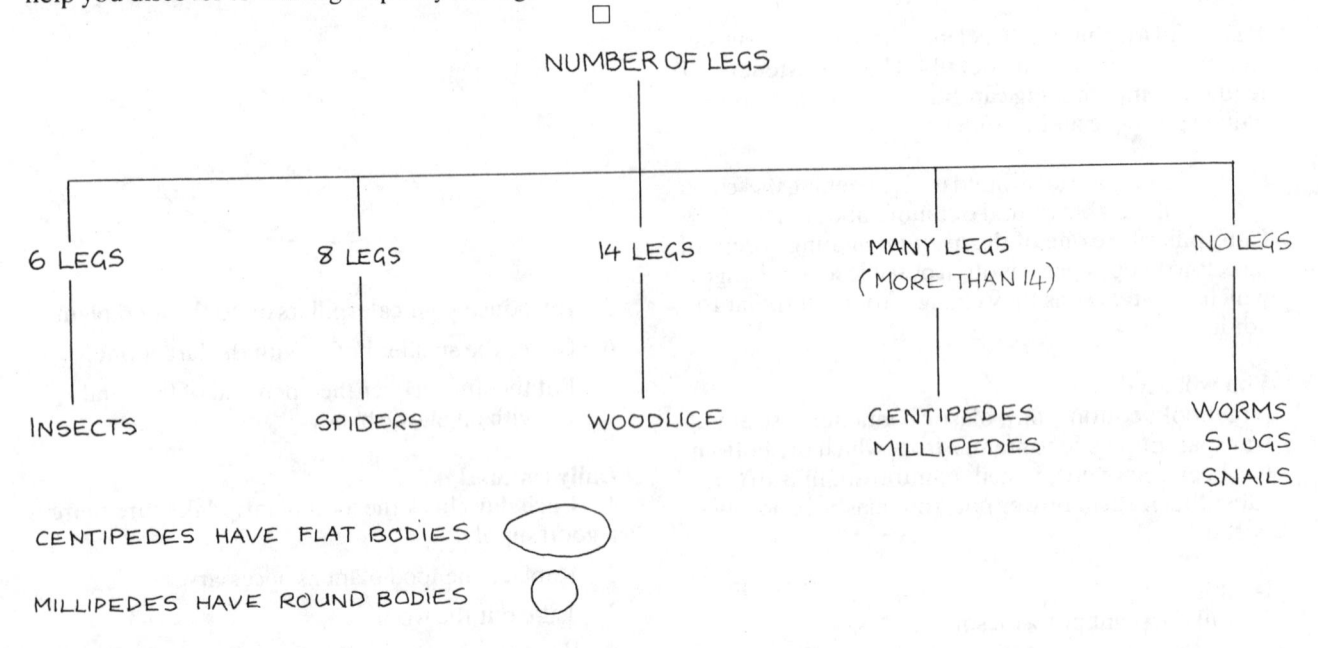

NUMBER OF LEGS

6 LEGS	8 LEGS	14 LEGS	MANY LEGS (MORE THAN 14)	NO LEGS
INSECTS	SPIDERS	WOODLICE	CENTIPEDES MILLIPEDES	WORMS SLUGS SNAILS

CENTIPEDES HAVE FLAT BODIES

MILLIPEDES HAVE ROUND BODIES

SPIDERS ARE CARNIVORES
WOODLICE ARE HERBIVORES
CENTIPEDES ARE CARNIVORES
MILLIPEDES ARE HERBIVORES
BIG BEETLES ARE CARNIVORES
ANTS ARE OMNIVORES

CATERPILLAR

HAS ONLY 3 PAIRS OF LEGS. THE LAST ARE PADS.

Assignment Number 22

Keeping Stick Insects

P We find it difficult observing many insects outside, because we only catch fleeting glimpses of most of them as they dash away to hide. Butterflies move as soon as we get close to them. Stick insects which are easy to keep, can be handled, and studied with relative ease. They can be fed on usually easily obtainable plants. By careful observations children should be able to discover a great deal about these interesting creatures. They should also learn a sense of discipline, remembering to clean them out, change their food, and so on.

C Most insects which we see in our travels are not easy to study in the wild state. Stick insects are easy to keep, they do not move very much, and we can study them in captivity. Unlike many wild insects, which are difficult to study, we should not have any trouble with the stick insects.

You will need
Glass container, muslin, stick insects (preferably species known as *Carausius morosus*), privet leaves (or if not available, holly or ivy), small bottle, cotton wool, notebook, pencil.

Do this
1. Arrange the privet in water in the small bottle.
2. Plug the top with cotton wool in case any of the insects fall in. Eggs might also fall into the water.
3. Place the small bottle of privet in the large container.
4. Introduce the stick insects. 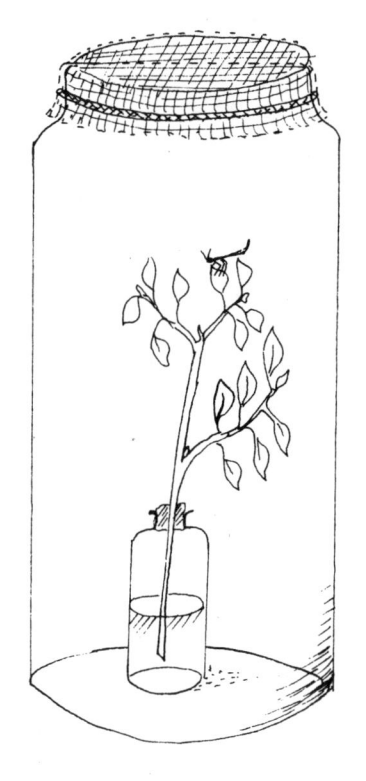
5. Cover the top with muslin and secure with the elastic band.
6. Make sure that they have a regular supply of fresh leaves. Although older insects can deal with holly and ivy, younger ones have less strong jaws — mandibles — and cannot do this.
7. Make sure that the container is cleaned out once a week.
8. You should make sure that you sort out the droppings from the eggs. Eggs are about the size of a match head. They are dark brown in colour, with a light yellow 'cap' to the egg.

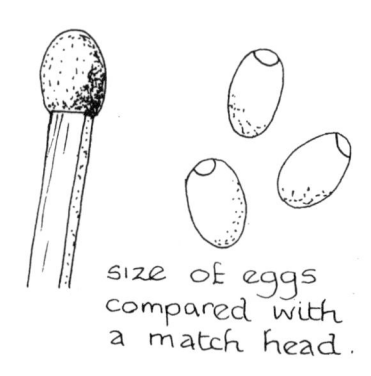

size of eggs compared with a match head.

9. Most stick insects are female. Few males are discovered. Female stick insects lay fertile eggs. When the females are young, they lay two or three every day. Less are laid as they get older.
10. Place the eggs in a separate container.
11. Watch them regularly and place suitable food inside once they hatch. It will take between four and six months for them to hatch — on average. Others may take much longer.

Think about this
1. Watch your stick insects over a period of time. There are only three stages in their life history. Discover what they are. How does this compare with most other insects?
2. Keep careful records of the time spent in each stage. Describe the different stages.
3. You could try and find out whether all your stick insects grow at the same rate. Why not place some in a warm place and some in a cold place? Do not have just one or two, but several in each situation, so that your observations will be more accurate.

Assignment Number 22

4 Try to discover how the stick insects grow, and at what speed. Keep careful records of your findings.

5 Look for changes taking place in the insects. Try to discover how much the insects grow when these changes take place.

6 Try to discover how the insect protects itself from its enemies.

Find out more
Look at other insects to discover what means of protection they have. How effective is each method? ☐

Looking at Snails

P & C Many common species of snails can be housed in simple homes, so that they can be studied more readily. It is surprising how little we know about even the most common species.

Snails are quite easy to find in most areas. They move very slowly, so that they can be studied readily. Simple houses can be made, and as long as they are fed regularly they should live in captivity quite happily for some time.

You will need
Aquarium (although you can use a large sandwich box), cover for the aquarium — (glass sheet, for example), cork, leaf litter and soil or sphagnum moss, small clump of grass, small plant pot for shelter (or similar), small stones, small jar, top, snails, warm water in a small dish, notebook, pencil, waterproof felt tip marker (fine point), paintbrush, sandpaper, ashes, sand, gravel.

Do this
1 Place some gravel in the bottom of the aquarium.
2 Dampen it well.
3 Add a layer of sphagnum moss to this, or soil and leaf litter.
4 Snails always need a damp home. Keep the aquarium in a warm, but not hot, place and put a small jar of water inside. It will remain humid. Make sure that the water is replaced as it evaporates. Cover the top of the water with a perforated cap.

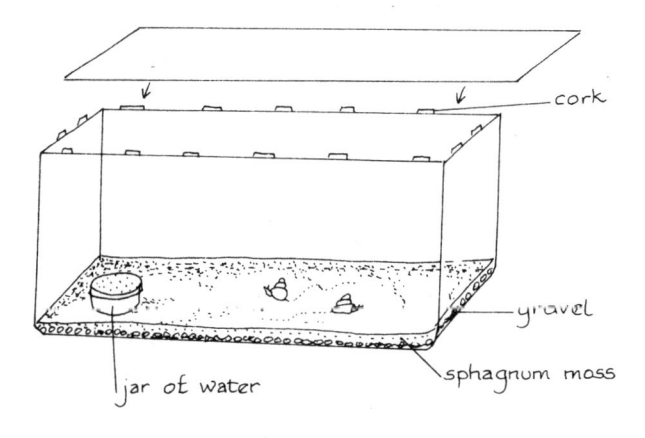

5 Cut the cork into a number of thin pieces. Place around the rim of the aquarium (fixing with glue if necessary), to allow air to circulate.
6 Place the glass lid in position.

Primary 3 and 4
Do this
1 Feeding your snails is quite easy. They eat plants.
2 To discover whether they have any preferences offer them as many different leaves as you can find. Some plants, especially members of the cabbage family, will smell, and so will the snails' waste matter.
3 Work out an investigation to discover how quickly your snails move.
4 Place a snail in a dish with a small amount of warm water. This will bring it out of its shell.
5 Dry the snail and place it on a piece of glass or perspex.
6 Once the snail has become attached to the glass, turn it upside down.
7 Watch how the snail moves.
8 Record your observations in your notebook.
9 Look where the snail has been on the glass. Can you see its slime trail? If you cannot see it very clearly, sprinkle the glass with talcum powder. Shake the glass, and the surplus powder will fall off, leaving the rest on the sticky trail.
10 Look at this trail very closely, and see how the snail moved. Was it in a straight line?
11 Can you think how the slime trail might help the snail to move? Think about why you need to have your bike oiled at intervals.

Primary 5 and 6
Do this
1 Place your snail on a piece of sandpaper. Record your observations. Make sure that you watch and listen.
2 Place your snail on some ashes or sand. Record your observations.

Observing snails feeding
1 When a snail is feeding look at its mouth through a hand lens. See if you can see its radula. Find out what this is.
2 Look at the leaf on which the snail has been feeding. See if you can discover how it attacked the leaf.
3 Place a number of different leaves away from the snail. See whether it makes its way towards them. If it does, see whether it has any preferences. You will need to repeat this with (a) the same snail and (b) different snails.
4 Record what you discover.

Assignment Number 23

Can a snail feel?
1 Try touching a snail's foot with a paintbrush.
2 Record its reaction.
3 Try shining a light onto the snail's tentacles.
4 What happens?

When do snails move about?
1 If you have snails living in the garden, you could try and discover when they move about.
2 Go out on a damp evening, and shine a torch around the garden. You should be able to see snails feeding. If it is too dry, they will not be out and about.
3 Have a similar chart to the one below to discover when snails are active.

	WET AND COLD		WET AND WARM	
Active	YES	NO	YES	NO

	DRY AND COLD		DRY AND WARM	
Active	YES	NO	YES	NO

Homing instincts
Snails are said to have strong homing instincts. You could try and discover whether they return to the same place.

1 Discover where your snails rest during the day. Look in very dark, damp places, such as under stones, flower pots, etc.

2 Place a small dot on the snail's shell using a fine dark coloured waterproof felt tip marker.

3 Visit different sites in your garden. Use a different colour for different places.

4 Draw a rough plan of your garden. Mark on it your snail sites. Also mark on it the colours you used to mark them from each particular site.

5 Regularly investigate your sites. You will need to go around the garden when it gets dark to see whether your snails are out. See how many of the marked ones you can see moving about.

6 If you have found your snails out feeding, you should make sure that you visit the garden early the following day to see whether they have returned.

Assignment Number 24

Further Studies with Earthworms

P & C Earthworms are easy to study, mainly because they do not move very quickly. These further studies will enable you to discover much more about these important creatures.

You will need
Earthworms, notebook, pencil, dish, microscope, test tube, cotton wool, sandpaper, notepaper, newspaper, glass, polythene.

Earthworms do not like being handled. You can look at one either by placing it in a dish under the microscope or in a test tube plugged with cotton wool.

Primary 3 and 4
Do this
Look at the body of your earthworm carefully. Can you see any divisions along the body? Can you see where they go? Can you find out the proper name for these divisions? We use the same names for divisions inside an orange.

Primary 5 and 6
Do this
1 Look at the body of your earthworm. Can you find which is the front end and which is the rear end?

2 Can you discover whether the earthworm has a head as such?

3 Can you see a mouth — think about food and feeding in your wormery and on your lawn.

4 Are there any eyes?

5 See if you can find a thicker area along the length of the body. This is the saddle, and is important when earthworms mate. It is important for making the cocoons to protect the earthworm's eggs.

6 Put your earthworm on different surfaces, and watch how it moves: try sandpaper, notepaper, newspaper, plastic, glass, and anything else you can find.

7 Watch carefully and record any sounds which you hear as the earthworm moves.

8 Do you notice whether the worm leaves a trail? If it does, what use do you think this trail has?

9 Look at the underside of the earthworm with your hand lens. Can you see the tiny bristles? What do you think the earthworm uses these for? Have you watched a blackbird or thrush trying to pull a worm out of the ground? Does it find it easy? Do you think these bristles help the worm in any way? Can you explain how?

Assignment Number 25

Discover how many Worms live in your Lawn

P & C If you have a lawn you will be able to discover something about the earthworm population there. Earthworms are active in the soil all the while. Sometimes it is easier to see this activity. Some species of earthworms leave small piles of soil, called worm casts, on the surface. They push this up, from below when making their tunnels. Not all worms do this. You could try and find out which species are responsible.

You will need
A ruler, tape measure, notebook, pencil, dish for the worm casts, weighing scale, four sticks.

Do this
1 Look for all the worm casts on your lawn.

2 Note down the numbers in your book.

3 Find the area of your lawn. Note this down in your notebook.

4 Now mark out a 50 cm square and use four sticks to mark the corners.

5 Take the casts inside and weigh them. This will give you an idea of how much soil the earthworms move.

Think about this
The following questions will help you to understand a little about the importance of earthworms in the soil.

1 From the number of worm casts discovered, how many worms live in a 50 square centimetre area of your lawn?

2 How many live in the whole of your lawn?

3 How much did your worm casts weigh for a 50 square centimetre area?

4 How much would the worm casts weigh for your complete lawn?

5 How much would the worm casts weigh in one hectare?

If you are feeling ambitious, you could collect worm casts for one week, to see how much soil the earthworms shift in this time. You will find that once you have cleared the casts, more will appear.

Adopt a Tree

P By looking at various aspects of a tree over a period of time it is possible to come to understand a great deal more about it. Questions such as 'What shape is it?' 'When did the first leaves appear?' etc can be answered by careful study and record keeping. After a period of time, a more complete picture of the chosen tree will emerge.

C You probably walk past trees quite often. Sometimes you might look at them because you notice something about them — there may be birds up in the branches, or leaves falling from them. By keeping regular careful records, you will soon be able to discover much more about your tree.

You will need
Recording board, paper, pencil, notebook, thick wax crayon (or heelball), microscope, hand lens, Blu-tack, card, clear book-covering material.

Do this
1   Look at the general shape of the tree. Make a sketch of the tree. If it is an awkward shape, use your hands to give you the feel. Start with your fingertips pointing at the top of your tree. Now spread these outwards, one in each direction to get the feel of the shape. This will help you to draw it much more easily.

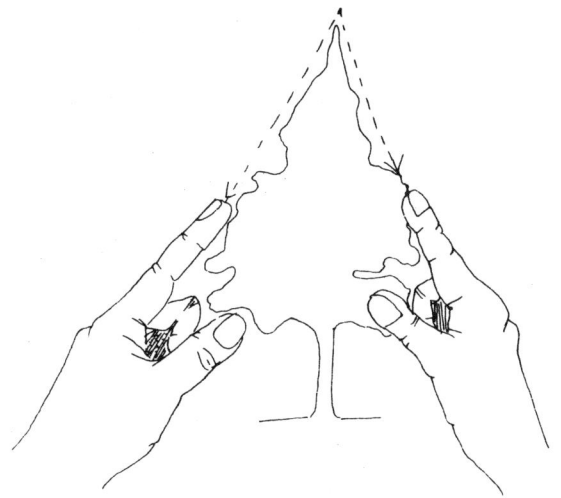

2   Try to describe the shape of your tree. Looking at it does it remind you of anything?

3   Does it grow out more at one side than another?

4   Is it an even shape?

5   Where is it growing? Look at the position of your tree. Describe it.

6   Is it growing on a slope such as a hillside?

7   Does it grow close to a stream?

8   Write down any other interesting things about where it is growing, such as whether there are other trees growing close by. If there are, are they the same or different species?

9   Describe the trunk. Is the trunk of your tree straight or is it twisted?

10   Does the trunk lean to one side or does it stand upright?

11   Where do the first branches come out?

12   Are they low down, or are they nearer the top?

13   Can you discover how far from the ground the lowest branch is?

14   Do you know the name given to the outer layer of the trunk?

15   Have a look at the bark. Is the bark rough or is it smooth?

16   Is there a pattern on the bark?

17   If there is, is it regular or irregular?

18   Can you write down some words to describe your bark?

19   Can you discover whether the bark is thick or thin? Do not take pieces off the tree — why not? You might find some pieces of bark on the ground. Take small pieces back with you and look at them under the microscope, or with a hand lens.

20   Look carefully at the colour of the bark. Is it the same all over?

21   Make a bark rubbing (see Assignment sheet 27).

22   Have a look at the leaves. What shape are they?

23   Are they all the same shape and size?

24   Make a leaf rubbing (as suggested below).

Leaf rubbings
Do this
1   To make a leaf rubbing, you do not need to pull a leaf off the tree.

2   Put your recording board under a leaf. This gives a firm surface.

3   Place a piece of plain paper on top of the leaf.

4   Rub all over the surface with a thick wax crayon, make sure that you keep each crayon stroke going in the same direction. As you do that you will have to take your hand off the paper after each completed stroke.

5   Cut out your leaf shapes and mount them with your other tree material.

6   In autumn collect different coloured leaves. Mount them on card and cover with book covering material. They will stay fresh, and keep their colours.

Assignment Number 27

Patterns in Bark

P & C We can recognise a tree from various parts of it. For example, we know one tree leaf is different from another. The shape of the tree will not be like the shape of another species. Each tree has its own bark pattern as well.

By collecting bark prints we can use these to help us identify trees at a later date.

You will also find details for making plaster casts of areas of bark (see Assignment Number 49). This is another way of keeping records of the different bark which you will come across in your travels. If you do a bark cast well, you can actually see the texture.

You will need
Notebook, pencil, thick (black) wax crayons, sheets of thin paper (about 15cm x 15cm), Blu-tack (or similar) or drafting tape, plaster of paris, plasticine, mallet, flat container like seed tray, water in bottle, mixing pot (e.g. yoghurt container), spoon, Assignment sheet 49.

Do this
1   Look carefully at the bark of the tree and select a suitable and typical area.

2   Fix the paper to the tree. You can use Blu-tack or, if the bark is fairly smooth, drafting tape. If you have neither of these, ask someone to hold it for you.

3   Put a 'T' for top at the top of your paper.

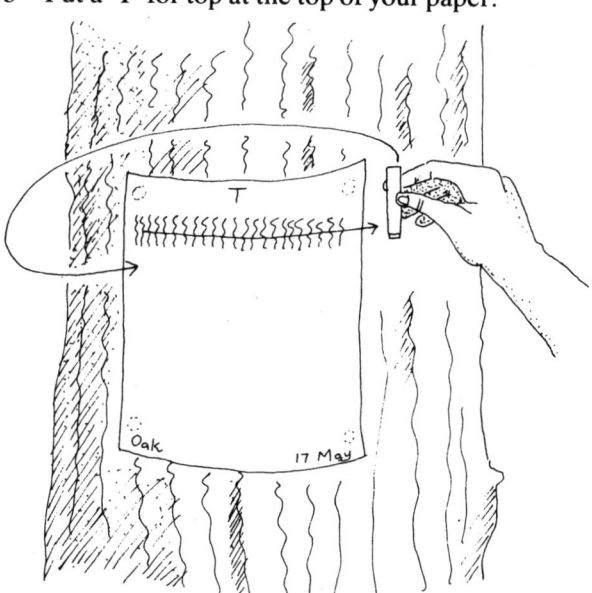

4   Gently rub over the paper with the side of the wax crayon. Make sure that each stroke goes in the same direction. That means you will have to take your hand off the paper after each stroke.

5   When you have completed your bark rubbing, cut it out, mount it alongside other information from your tree.

6   If you can find the same species of tree of different ages, complete several bark rubbings for comparison.

Think about this
1   Look at different parts of the trunk of the same tree to see whether there are different areas of bark.

2   Look at young and old trees of the same species — and middle-aged ones if you can find them. Is the bark the same? Does it change?

Make a Plaster Cast
Do this
1   Flatten out a piece of plasticine (about 7-10 cm across).

2   Hold this against a suitable area of bark.

3   Hit the plasticine with a mallet or your fist.

4   Carefully peel away the plasticine.

5   You should have a good impression of your bark in the plasticine.

6   Place this in a flat tray so that you do not damage it.

7   Refer to Assignment sheet 49 for making a plaster cast.

27a

How Old is That Tree?

P Discovering the age of a tree is not always easy. The only accurate way to find out how old a tree is is to cut it down and count the annual rings. However, since this is not practicable, there is a rough guide for finding the age of deciduous (hardwood) trees. Deciduous trees lose their leaves in winter. Evergreen trees, including the majority of conifers, keep their leaves all the year round. They lose some gradually all the while.

Youngsters can use this rough method for finding the age of their deciduous trees.

C Sometimes you can tell if a tree is old — perhaps it is big, or the bark is cracking or it may have died. But it isn't always easy to tell exactly how old a tree is. In fact the only way we can do this is to count the annual rings when the tree has died and is felled. Each of these rings tells us how much the tree grew that year. By counting these rings we can tell how old the tree is. There is a simple way of telling roughly how old a deciduous tree is whilst it is still standing.

You will need
Notebook, pencil, tape measure.

Do this
1 Although trees do not grow at exactly the same rate, a well known tree expert, Alan Mitchell, has found that an average hardwood tree grows about 2.5cm each year.

2 Measure your tree at 1.5m above the ground.

3 Put your tape measure round the tree to find the distance all the way round. This is called the girth. You will need to have someone to help you hold the tape measure.

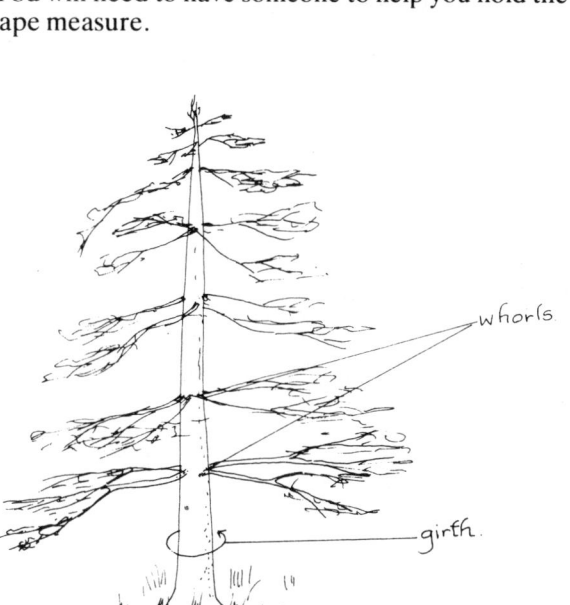

4 Divide your result by 2.5.

5 This will give you the age of the tree.
It is easier to tell the age of conifers (like fir trees). You count the circles (whorls) of branches.

6 Count the whorls of your fir trees and other conifers to find the age.

Think about this
1 Try and find hardwood trees and conifers about the same age. Compare their girths and heights. (For heights, see Assignment sheet 30.)

Primary 5 and 6
1 Make a list of differences between trees.
2 Make a list of uses for various types of wood.

Assignment Number 28

28 a

Assignment Number 29

Looking at Leaves

P Although the leaves on some trees vary in shape and size — and it is useful to look at these — individual species of trees have leaves which help us to recognise the tree. Learning to recognise trees, sort out leaves, etc., is a useful exercise, since it teaches children to make careful observations.

C Leaves are very important to trees. You will see that where a leaf joins the main stem there is always a bud.

Primary 3 and 4
You will need
A variety of leaves, pencil, paper.

1 Put all your leaves together and sort them into two sets, called simple leaves and compound leaves. We have drawn some to show you. Simple leaves are made up of one main part, even though this might be divided. Compound leaves are made up of leaflets.

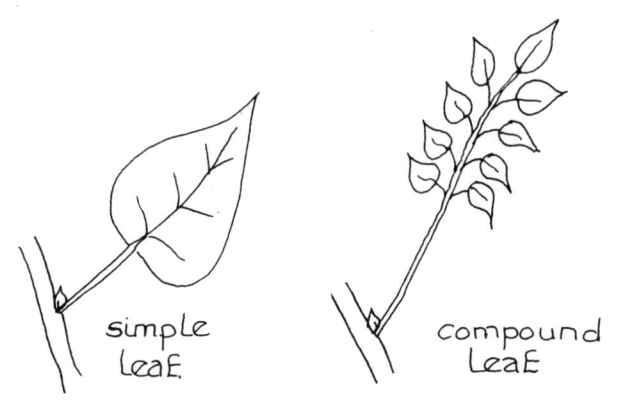

2 Put together the leaves from the same tree. Draw the outlines of these to show the different shapes of leaves from the same tree.

Primary 5 and 6

1 Use a collection of leaves, but divide them up in the following way.

2 Hold up various leaves to the light. You will see that they have veins.

3 Look very closely at these. You will see that the veins of different leaves are arranged differently. You should see that some veins are much bigger than others. These are the main veins.

4 Now try to arrange your leaves in sets according to the arrangement of the veins.

5 You should find two vein arrangements:
(a) net veined leaves have veins which spread out from the main vein like a net.

(b) Parallel-veined leaves have veins which run almost side by side without branching.

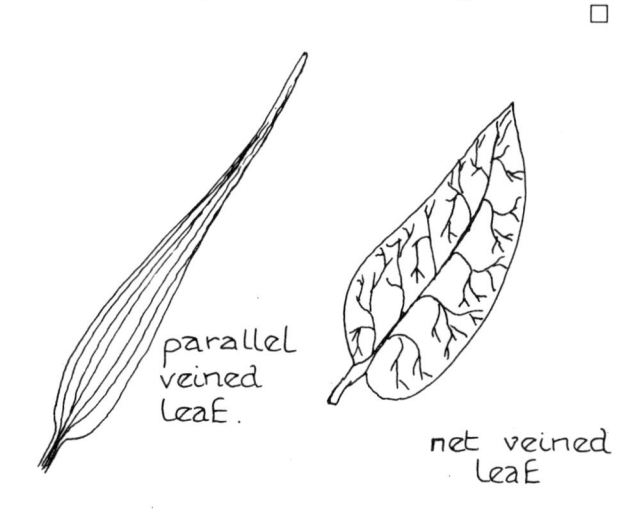

Assignment Number 30

Estimating and Measuring Tree Heights

P Young children find it difficult to estimate the heights of objects like trees, but it is valuable for them to be able to do so. Estimating is a useful exercise which, although it may not be applied until later in life, gives children an insight into how far things are away, and so on. In this Assignment we look at heights of trees using various techniques for estimating and measuring. The method, once mastered, can be used for other measuring activities — e.g. buildings.

C There are several ways of measuring trees without cutting them down. You can try some of these.

You will need
Pencil, notebook, stick about 2m long, protractor, 2 small screws, piece of hardboard, length of string, piece of plasticine, mathematical tables, compass (directional), sticks, measuring tape chalk.

Primary 3 and 4
Do this
The Pencil Method will give you an accurate estimate of the height of a tree. If you can persuade several people to do it for the same tree, with each writing down the results, you can compare these.

1 You will need a friend to help you.

2 Hold the pencil vertically in front of you at arm's length.

3 Move backwards until the bottom of your pencil is lined up with the bottom of the tree trunk, and the top of the pencil is level with the top (crown) of the tree.

4 Once you have done this, stay where you are.

5 Turn your pencil horizontal so that the base of the pencil appears to be at the base of the tree.

6 Instruct your friend to walk away from the tree. He will have to walk away at right angles to an imaginary line between you and the tree. He should keep walking until he appears to arrive at the end of the pencil.

7 Now put a stick in the ground where he is standing.

8 Pace out, or measure with a tape, the distance from the base of the tree to the stick. This distance should be the same as the height of your tree.

Primary 5 and 6
The Stick Method is another simple method, and works for trees up to 20m.

1 You will need someone to help you.

2 From the trunk walk 27 paces away from the tree. It is important that you try and keep each of your strides the same length. How long they are is not important.

3 Give your stick to your partner to hold at the 27 pace spot.

4 You now need to walk a further three paces from the stick.

5 Make a mark on the ground here.

6 Now lie down on the ground with one eye as close to the ground as you can get it.

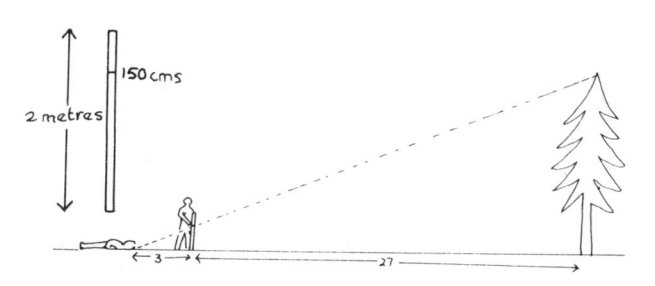

30 a

Assignment Number 30

7 In this position look towards the top of the tree, making sure that you can see your stick and your friend.

8 Your partner has to move his finger up and down the stick.

9 You tell him to stop when his finger is at the same height as the top of the tree — as you look at it.

10 Your partner makes a mark on the stick with a piece of chalk.

11 To find the height of the tree measure the distance from the ground to the chalk mark and multiply this by ten. If the mark on the stick is 60cm from the ground, then the height of the tree is 60cm x 10 = 600cm = 6m.

Primary 5 and 6
Using a clinometer
Do this

1 You can use a clinometer which measures angles, to discover the height of a tree more accurately. You could also use this method and compare the results with estimates obtained using other methods.

2 Make a clinometer from the protractor, piece of hardboard, string, plasticine and screws, as shown in the illustration.
To make the instrument easier to hold, you could carve some hand holds.

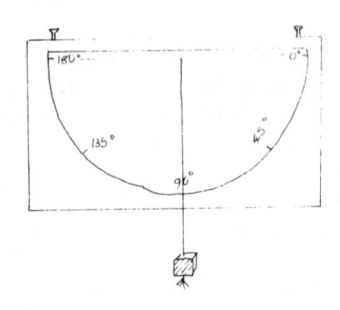

3 Walk backwards from the tree holding the clinometer, as shown in the illustration. Continue walking until the screws are lined up with the top of the tree.

4 With the screws lined up, continue walking backwards until your plumb line hangs at an angle of 45°. Stop now, and you will have enough information to find the height of the tree.

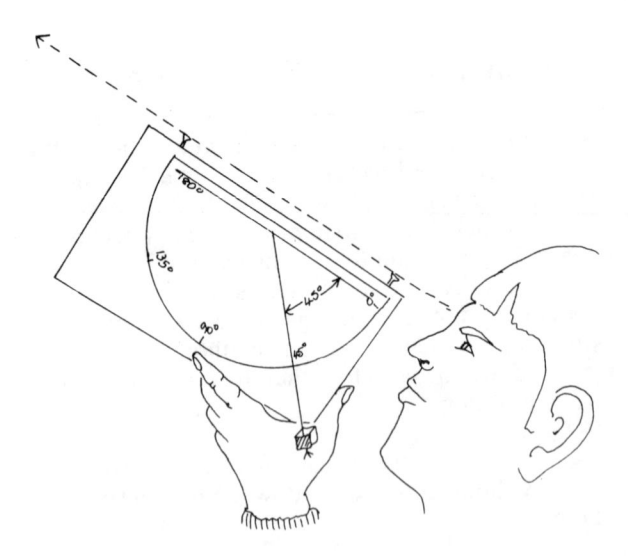

5 To do this you will need to use some mathematical tables. Your tree height is equal to your distance from the tree, plus your own eye-level height.

6 To find this we have to use a simple formula. On our diagram 'a' is the length from you to the tree, and 'b' is the angle which you read off on the clinometer, and 'c' is the height from your feet to your eyes.

The height of the tree = $c + (a \times \tan b)$

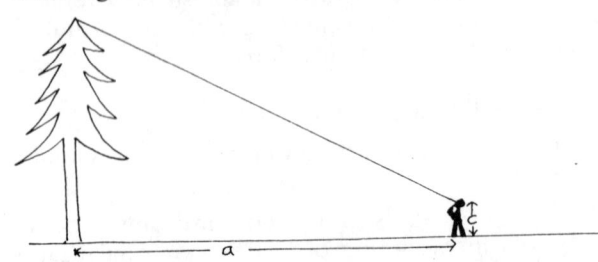

7 Look up tan b (= 45°) in your tables. Using an angle of 45° makes the working out easy, but you will not always be able to do this with awkwardly shaped trees.

Primary 5 and 6
Looking at the tree canopy

You can discover much about your tree by looking at your tree canopy. The canopy is the area covered by the branches and leaves. You will need someone to help you.

Do this

1 Make a simple chart in your notebook for recording the information.

Direction	Distance
North	
North East	
East	
South	
South East	
South West	
West	
North West	

Assignment Number 30

2   Use your compass to find North.

3   Walk out to the edge of the canopy in this northerly direction. Put a stick in the ground where you reach the edge.

4   Use the tape measure to measure the distance.

5   Record this in your chart against 'North'.

6   Repeat this for all the other compass points.

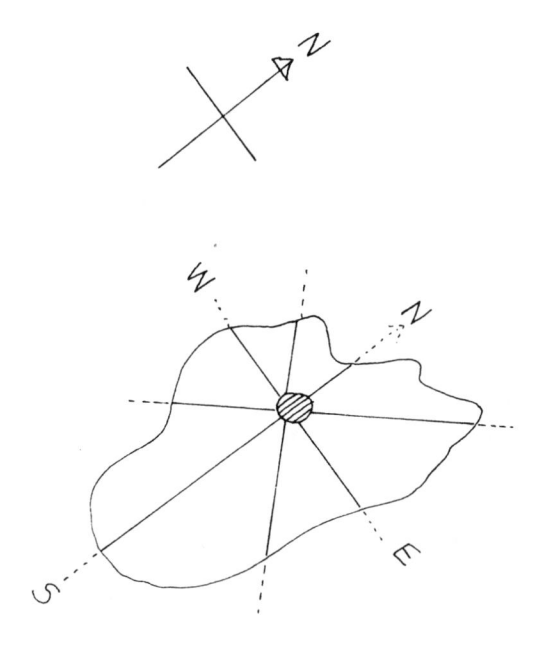

direction	distance
N	3 metres
NE	9 metres
E	5½ metres
SE	7½ metres
S	12 metres
SW	5½ metres
W	4½ metres
NW	3½ metres

7   Before you leave, by standing under your tree you will be able to see whether it spreads out more in one direction than another. You will be able to confirm this by looking at your figures in the chart.

Think about this
Can you discover any reasons why there might be a wider spread on one side than another?
   For example, are there other trees growing close by?
   Is there rock on one side?
   Does the tree grow on a slope?

Assignment Number 31

Keeping Small Mammals

P Where possible small children should be encouraged to keep small mammals as pets. There are many reasons for this. Although tame, captive animals behave differently from their wild relatives, nevertheless children are able to discover much about them. Studying captive animals at close quarters will enable them to find out more about their behaviour, what they require, and so on. Food preferences can be discovered, details about the number of young born, and so forth will be forthcoming if the animals are kept for long enough.

It should be possible to capitalise on the keeping of small mammals. We have made some suggestions here about keeping small mammals, and ways in which they can be observed.

It is important that only the 'tried and tested' mammals are kept. Do not buy exotic creatures, and this is especially true in areas where wild animals are captured and sold for 'pets'. Most will be very unhappy in confined spaces and will often die very quickly.

It is everyone's duty to emphasise to their youngsters that wild animals belong in the wild state, and not in small cages.

In encouraging children to keep pets, we should be aiming at a humane attitude. We should encourage children to care for their creatures, and to look after them properly. If it is possible that such ideas may not, or cannot be put into practice successfully, then it is best not to keep these small mammals.

Designing cages is a good exercise in planning and discussion with the child, although the parent will usually have to do the building. Discussion should take place about size, sleeping quarters, shelter, etc. It is perhaps best to refer the reader to a recognised book — (see Practical Book of Pet Keeping in book list).

C Keeping small animals is fun, because we can learn so much about them. But because we have decided to keep them we have a responsibility towards them. Small mammals are like us. They need to be looked after. They need to be fed, cleaned out, etc regularly. You would not like to go without your food or without water. If you decide that you want to keep these small mammals — creatures like hamsters, gerbils etc — then you must decide to look after them. They need to be fed regularly, they need to be cleaned out regularly, they need to be looked at frequently to make sure that they are well. Think about these things before you decide whether you want the responsibility. The thought of having a pet is fun — but it doesn't always last.

You will need
An aquarium (which is suitable for the keeping of small mammals) or a bought/home made cage, zinc top (if aquarium is used), weights (if aquarium is used), small box for shelter/sleeping quarters or, in the case of hamsters, jam jar, bedding, e.g. sawdust, hay, food and water containers, food, notebook, pencil.

Do this
When we talk about 'the cage' it can be the aquarium, or a proper cage.

1 Arrange the bedding on the floor of the cage.

2 Put in a shelter — a small box or a jar which will give the creature privacy. Some mammals, like hamsters, like to have a bedroom in which to sleep. Turn the jar on its side, and put in some bedding, wood, shredded paper (not newspaper) is suitable.

3 Cut the zinc to fit the top of the aquarium. Once the animal is inside, hold the zinc cover in place with weights.

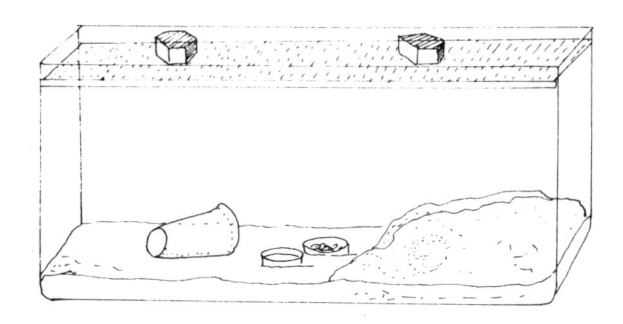

4 Introduce your small mammal into its new home.

5 Allow it to settle in. Although you should talk to it, and be friendly towards it, do not disturb it or frighten it too much until it has settled in.

6 Keep your cage in a cool place.

7 Make sure that your animal is fed and cleaned out regularly. Keep a careful check on your cage to see that it doesn't get too hot. If you are using an aquarium, you might have problems in very hot conditions. Check the inside temperature with a thermometer. You might know that conditions are getting rather uncomfortable for your animal if you see condensation on the inside of your tank. If this happens or the internal temperature does get too hot, make sure that you move your small mammals to a cooler place. Directing the cold air from a fan onto/into the aquarium might solve the problem on a short-term basis. Try and check whether this problem is likely to occur **before** you buy your mammal.

All small mammals are different, but the following will help you to find out more about your pet.

31a

Assignment Number 31

Think about this
1 What sort of food does it prefer?
2 How does it eat?
3 Does it chew, gnaw or tear at its food?
4 Does it drink much?
5 Is it nocturnal?
6 How long does it sleep?
7 Is it about all day?
8 If it is nocturnal, do you think it is about all night?
9 How does it move?
10 If you have more than one small mammal, try to ensure that you have a male and a female, so that you can breed them. If you do, how many young are there in a litter?
11 Find out as much as you can about the young. Do not disturb the mother too much. Some small mammals will eat their offspring, if they think there is danger.
12 If you have more than one, do they fight with each other?

Assignment Number 32

One Square Metre

P & C Few of us realise the changes which take place around us. We are seldom aware of what happens, not only as the seasons change, but from day to day and week to week. It is difficult studying large areas, but by making a regular study of one square metre, and keeping records, it is possible to discover what changes take place even within a small area. Changes here can be compared with changes which can be seen on the walk.

The square metre should be situated somewhere along the walk if this is possible. If not, choose a place near home to make regular visits possible.

You will need
String, four small stakes, mallet/hammer, notebook, pencil, ruler, tape.

Do this
1 Find a suitable place and stake out a square metre.

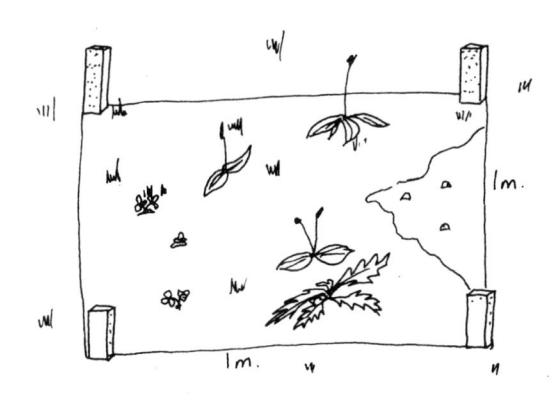

2 Make at least one regular weekly visit, more often if you want to. Keep a written record of what you find.

3 Once a month draw your square and record everything you find. Keep careful records of other things — temperatures, cloud cover, and so on (see Weather Assignments 5, 6 & 7 for further details).

Think about this
By studying your square metre once a week, you will soon be able to discover what changes are taking place. See if you can link the changes with the different seasons, different weather conditions, etc.

Primary 5 and 6
Do this
1 Carefully map on to a sheet of paper exactly what you find in your square once a month.

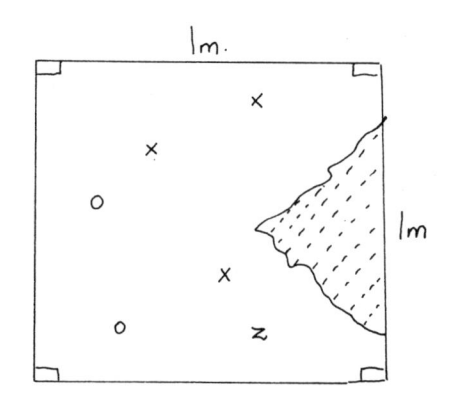

key: x plantain
o clover
z thistle
bare ground

Assignment Number 33

An Outdoor Plot

P **Make your own rock garden**

Children can discover the world about them on their walks. They also need to become involved closer at hand, to be able to create their own things. If you live in a suitable area you might be able to collect rocks for your rock garden which Primary 5 and 6 could do. Primary 3 and 4 can create their own smaller version.

C Making your own rock garden can be fun. You can do it in quite a small area.

You will need
Soil, coarse peat, a terracotta pan 30-35 cm across, broken crocks, plants. If you cannot buy a terracotta pan. use a plastic one, although this is less satisfactory, because terracotta is porous.

Do this
1. Can you find out what porous means?

2. Make sure that the pan has drainage holes in the bottom. Several smaller holes are better than one large one. These holes are important because they let any excess water drain away.

3. You will need to spread 'crocks' on the bottom of the pan, otherwise once the peat is put in, this will be washed out, either when we water the container (if we keep it inside) or when it gets rained on. Crocks consist of broken pieces of pot, small stones, etc.

4. Put about 1cm of coarse peat (or if you have them rotted leaves) into the bottom of the pot on top of the crocks.

5. Now fill almost to the top with soil.

6. Select a number of rock plants. Choose different varieties so that you will have a number to study. Plant half a dozen or so in your pot.

7. Keep careful records.

Think about this
1. How much does each plant grow (a) in a week (b) in a month?

2. Do some plants grow more quickly than others?

3. (a) When does it flower — if it does?
   (b) Do all kinds of plants flower at the same time?

Making a Large Rock Garden
You can make a bigger rock garden using a large container, such as an old sink. This will give more scope for experimenting for example with (a) different plants and (b) different areas — e.g. wet and dry.

You will need
An old sink or similar container, rock plants, peat, stone chippings, soil, notebook, stone for support, rocks for decoration, crocks. You will need to decide where you want your garden situated, since it will be heavy to move (almost impossible!) when it is full.

1. Position the 'trough'.
2. Use the larger stones to tilt the trough slightly.
3. Put some crocks in the bottom.
4. Cover these with a layer of coarse peat.
5. Put in a layer of soil to within 10cm of the top.
6. Press this down firmly.
7. Put in some more soil to within 1cm of the top.
8. Arrange one or two small rocks on the surface.
9. Arrange your plants. Remember that with your trough tilted one end will be damp and the other end drier. Don't forget that those plants which need drier conditions will need to be positioned at the drier end.

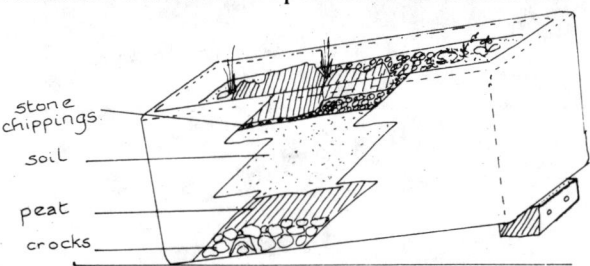

10. Put stone chippings over the surface of the soil. Not only will this help to keep the surface cool, but it will also stop the moisture from escaping, especially in spring time.

11. Keep your trough watered. Don't forget that those plants at the drier end may need soaking more often, if the water drains to the wetter end.

Think about this
1. Keep careful records of the development of your rock garden.

2. Which plants grow the quickest?

3. Which plants grow the most?

4. If you keep a regular weekly record of the growth of all or some of your plants, you could plot the results on a graph. You will have to decide how best to measure your plants. You might take the measurement across them, their height, number of flowers, etc. Whatever you do, have a page in your notebook so that you will be able to record accurately and consistently.

Assignment Number 34

Looking at Flowers

P Most flowers have a basic make-up. By looking carefully at one or two simple examples, it is possible to understand how a flower 'works', and how important it is for the plant.

C Have you ever looked carefully at a flower to see how it is made up? Do you know what each of the parts does? Now is your chance to discover something about this part of a plant.

You will need
Notebook, pencil, plain paper, hand lens, common flower — like a buttercup or a wallflower.

1 Look at your flowers using your hand lens.

2 Draw what you can see.

3 When you have done that, compare the parts which you have found with the drawing. Don't look until you have drawn yours — no cheating!

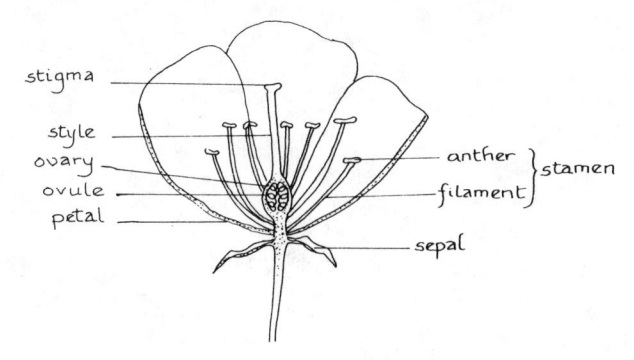

Think about this
1 Look up in a book what each of the parts does.

Find out more
1 Try and discover whether all flowers are like the ones which you have been looking at.

2 Have a look at Assignment sheet 35 which is about insect visitors to flowers.

34 a

Assignment Number 35

Insect Visitors to Flowers

P Flowers are visited regularly by a variety of insects. They either alight to rest, or they come for food. Occasionally some might find shelter in amongst the flower heads of some species. This project will help Primary 4 and 5 to see that insects visit flowers, and to discover some of the species. Primary 5 and 6 will be able to spend further time watching various flowers to obtain further information.

You will need
Notebook, pencil, small polythene bags, small tubes for collecting specimens, thread, pooter, elastic bands.

Do this
To help you with this survey, see if you can answer the following question **before** you begin:

1 Do insects come to flowers?

2 If they do, can you think of a reason why they might visit them?

3 What sort of flowers do insects visit?

All your information needs to be kept together. You will need to compare it at a later date. You will need to use the following information for each kind (species) of plant which you are looking at.
If your project is going to be successful you will need to watch **carefully** and **quietly.** When choosing flowers find some bright ones and some dull ones.

1 Choose a flower which you want to watch.

2 Position yourself near to it. You can sit down if you find it more comfortable or you can stand.

3 Do not disturb any insects which might arrive.

4 Make a list of all the insects which visit the flowers you are watching.

5 Once you have collected your information you should be able to answer the following questions.

Think about this
1 Do insects visit flowers?

2 Which sort of flowers do they visit?

3 Do they prefer brightly coloured ones to dull ones?

4 Why do the insects come to the flowers?

5 While you have been watching your flowers, have you seen other insects about, which do not visit flowers?

6 Are there different sorts of insects which visit the flowers?

Primary 5 and 6
When you looked at your flowers earlier, do you think that there might have been some animals on the flowers which you could not see?

You can carry out an investigation to try and answer this question. Before you start read these instructions carefully.

Do this
1 Place a small polythene bag over the head (flower) of a common plant.

2 Secure it with thread, but do not tie it too tightly, otherwise you may cut through the plant stem.

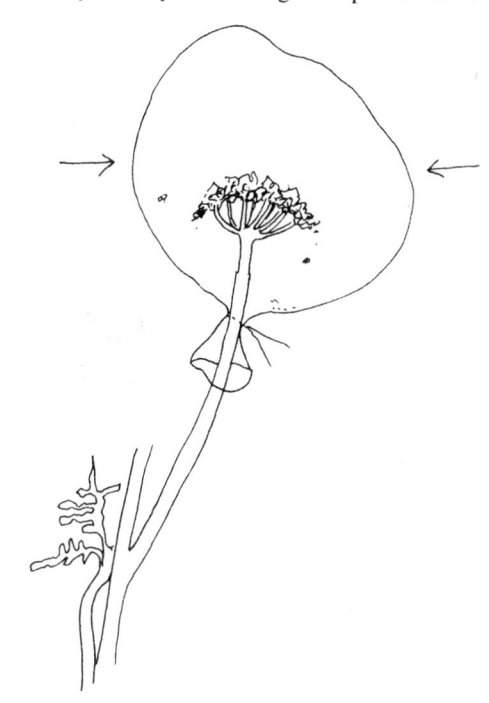

3 You do not need to remove the flower head, but instead shake it carefully but sharply. This should dislodge any animals which are there.

35 a

Assignment Number 35

4 Carefully untie the thread and take off the polythene bag.

5 Try to ensure that the animals which are inside do not escape.

6 Secure the top of the bag with an elastic band. You can take out the anmimals using a pooter (see Assignment sheet 19 for details). Put them in a specimen tube.

7 Make sure that each tube bears a label, giving the following important information:

   Name of flower
   Where collected
   Name of collector
   Date collected

8 You can use your hand lens to look at them now, and try to identify them. Or you can take them back home.

9 Take back only one of each species. Return the others to the flower heads.

Think about this

1 Can you think of any reasons why these smaller animals might be on the flower heads?

2 You could look to see whether they have done any damage to the flower.

3 If you covered a complete flower, and introduced some of these creatures, you would soon be able to see whether any damage was done.

4 Do these animals come here all the while?

5 Can you think up an investigation to find out whether the creatures are just visitors or whether they are there all the while?

□

Assignment Number 36

Looking at Seed Dispersal

P It would be of little use if the plant only produced seeds, and then did nothing with them. The dispersal of the seeds is very important if the species is to continue to grow. Dispersal varies, but by collecting seeds and looking at them, it is possible to understand something about the many ingenious methods of dispersal.

C Have you ever wondered how some plants, like the common weeds which grow in our gardens got there? We have seen that flowers produce seeds, but this would not be much use, if they did not do something with them.

The way in which plants spread their seeds varies from one kind of plant to another. We call the spreading of seeds 'dispersal'. We are going to look at some of the methods which plants use.

You will need
Seeds from Assignment sheet 37, other seeds, notebook, pencil.

Do this
There are three ways in which seeds are spread — dispersed. These are:- by wind, explosion, and by animals. (A few are dispersed by water.)

Seeds dispersed by:—

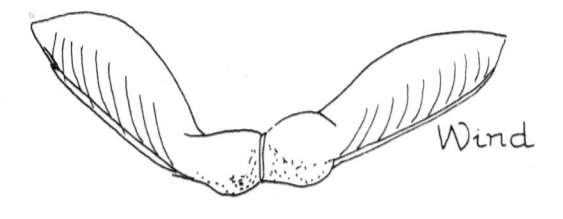

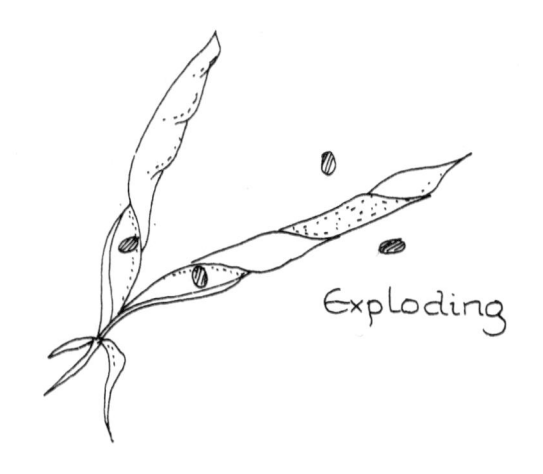

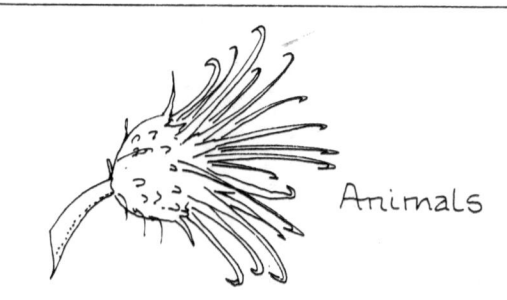

Wind

Exploding

Animals

1 Look at your seeds and try to discover ways in which animals can disperse seeds.

Think about this

1 See if you can find different sorts of seeds which are dispersed by the wind.

2 Some plants have 'explosive' methods for dispersing their seeds. Can you find the names of some of these?

Primary 5 and 6
Do this

1 Try to discover how your dispersed seeds grow.

2 See if you can find how long it takes for them to begin to germinate.

3 Collect the seeds from common species, like shepherd's purse. Count the seeds from a number of plants. See whether it varies. Try and grow as many as you can.

Think about this

1 What do you think is the most effective means for dispersing seeds?

2 Are some methods better than others? Why is this?

3 Did you find that some plants produce a lot more seeds than others? If they do, do you think there is a good reason for this?

Assignment Number 37

Looking at Fruits and Seeds

After flowers have been fertilized, fruits develop and these contain the seeds, so that new plants will be produced next year. The fruits vary. In some, like the plum, they are large: in others much smaller. All plants produce different sorts of seeds, and we can investigate these.

Once the flowers have been pollinated, the flower head dies off as the seeds develop.

You will need
Dying flower heads, notebook, pencil, hand lens.

Do this

1 Look at the different flower heads to discover where and how the seeds are developing.

2 Draw the different kinds of seeds.

3 Keep the seeds, as you can use them for Assignment sheet 36.

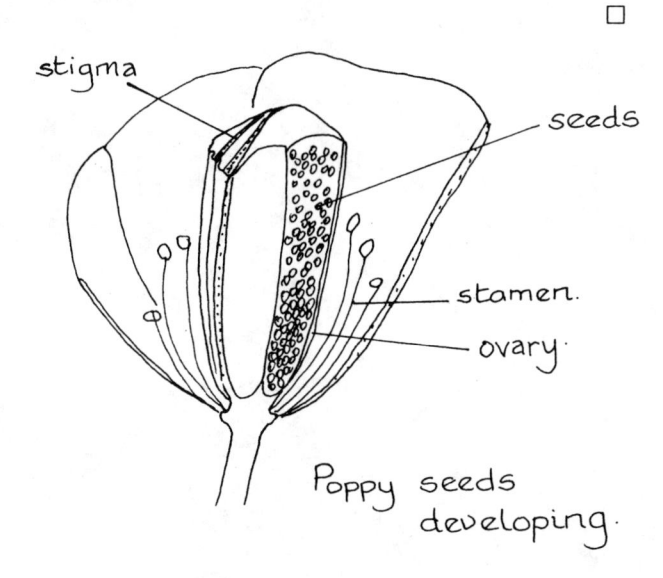

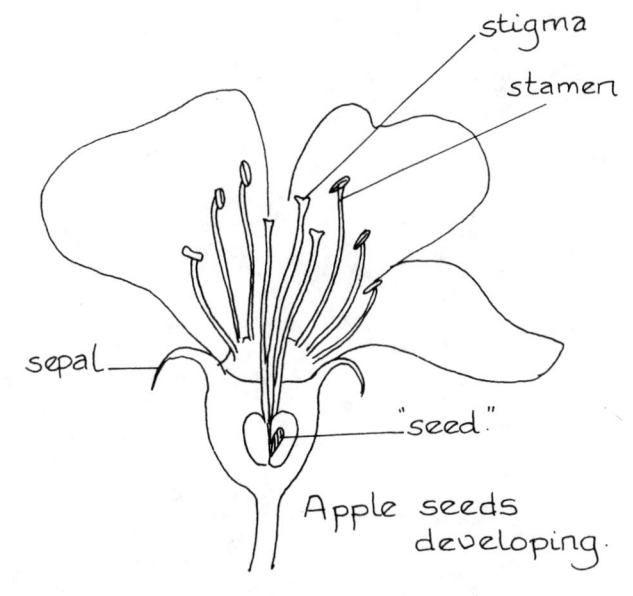

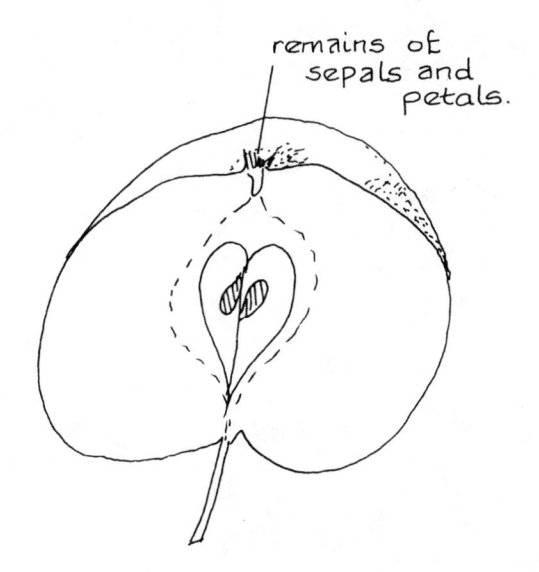

Assignment Number 38

Conditions for Seed Germination

P & C During your wanderings you will probably come across some kinds of seeds. If you do not discover the seeds of wild species, you might purchase seeds so that you can grow plants in your garden — if you have one — or in the house.

If you are not able to do this now, you can remember the time, when you did it 'back home'. We want you to try and discover whether there are certain conditions when seeds will or will not grow.

You will need
Cress seeds, cotton wool (or sawdust or peat), 4 jam jars (or similar containers), 4 labels, notebook, pencil.

Do this
1 Take some cotton wool (or sawdust or peat), and place a piece in the bottom of each jam jar.

2 Label the jars A, B, C and D.

3 Moisten the material in the bottom of jars A, B and C — but **not** in D.

4 Sprinkle some cress seeds onto the material in the bottom of the jars.

5 Place jars A and D on a window ledge — but not in direct sunlight, otherwise it might cause a fire!

6 Put B in the refrigerator.

7 Put C in an oven at a temperature of about 133°C for 30 minutes each day for five days. Then place with the others.

8 Leave the other jars for several days.

9 Water A, B and C regularly.

10 Draw a record sheet in your notebook similar to the one below:

Date	JAR A	JAR B	JAR C	JAR D
Monday 17th May	TODAY I PLANTED ALL THE SEEDS WITH — Water Light Room warmth	Water No Light except when fridge is open No warmth	Water Light Heat at first then room warmth	No water Light Room warmth
Wednesday 19th May	Seeds are splitting and a white root is	Nothing has happened	Nothing	Nothing

11 Look at all four jars regularly.

12 Record your observations. For example, if seeds started to grow write this in the correct column. If there was no change record this as well.

Think about this
1 Which seeds have begun to germinate? Look at your record sheet in your notebook in which you have recorded your observations.

2 If any seeds are growing, in which jars are they?

3 From your observations can you answer the following questions?

   (a) Did the seeds in Jar A with water germinate?

   (b) Did the seeds in D without water germinate?

   (c) Did the seeds in B in the cold germinate?

   (d) Did the seeds in C in hot conditions germinate?

   (e) What can you say about temperature and germination?

   (f) Can you make any comments about water and germination?

   (g) From your investigations which have led to observations, are there any conditions necessary for germination to take place? If there are, you should be able to name them.

38 a

Assignment Number 39

Seeds Grow Towards the Light

P Plants need light to grow properly. Plants also need light provided by the sun to make food by the process known as photosynthesis. Photo means 'light'; synthesis means 'to make'. Photosynthesis is the making of food in the presence of sunlight.

There is a simple investigation which will show that seeds grow towards the light.

C Plants have to make their own food. They need sunlight to do this. Seeds will grow towards the light. You can discover this, and see what happens when you reverse the light source.

You will need
A terracotta plant pot, blotting paper, cress seeds, margarine tubs, box to cover the tubs, notebook, pencil, saucer.

Do this
1 Moisten a piece of blotting paper and put it on the inside of a flower pot. It will stay there because it is wet.

2 Sprinkle some cress seeds onto the blotting paper.

3 Turn the plant pot upside down, and place it on a saucer of water.

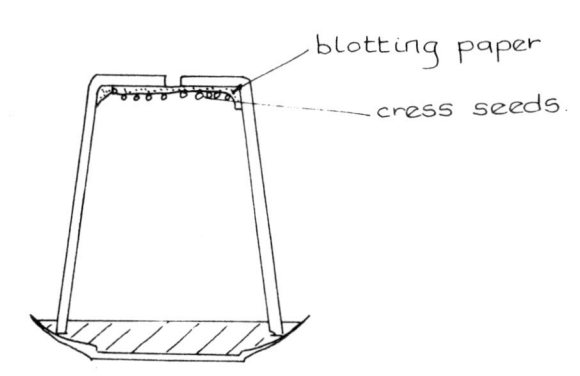

4 Keep a record of what happens.

Think about this
1 What happened to the seedlings under the plant pot?

Do this
1 Put some cotton wool, absorbent kitchen paper or a paper towel into the bottom of two margarine tubs.

2 Moisten the material.

3 Sprinkle some cress seeds here.

4 Cut a small hole in the side of a cardboard box.

5 Leave one margarine tub in the open. Put the other under the cardboard box.

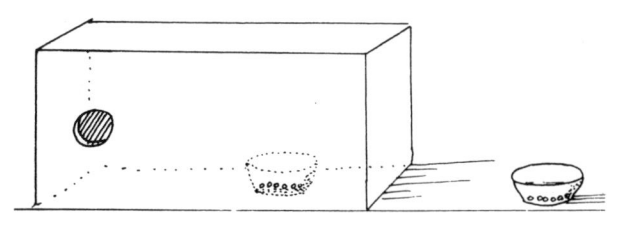

6 Compare the way in which the seeds grow.

7 Leave one margarine tub in the open.

8 Change the box round, so that the hole is now on the opposite side to which it was.

9 Keep careful records.

Think about this
1 What did you notice about the seeds which were not covered up?

2 What did you notice about the seeds where light was coming through the hole?

3 What did you notice when you changed the box round?

Looking at Bulbs Growing

P & C Because bulbs have enough food stored in them, they will grow without soil. By placing them in water, growth can be watched.

You will need
Glass container, bulb, notebook, pencil, water.

Do this
1 Fill the bottle with water.
2 Place the bulb on the top, ensuring that it is touching the water, otherwise it will not grow.

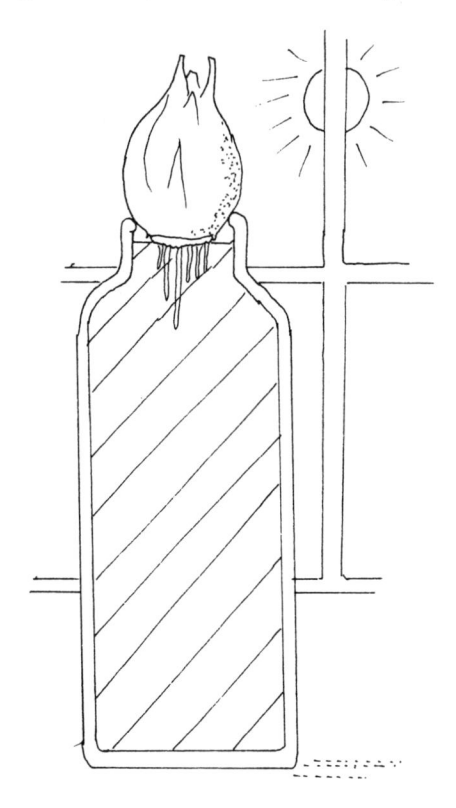

3 Keep careful records of what is happening.
4 Make sure that you place the container in a light window.
5 Make sure that the bulb is always touching the water.

Think about this
1 Why do you think bulbs are planted in soil if they can grow without it?

Primary 5 and 6
Find out more
1 See what you can find out about hydroponics.
2 See if you can grow plants using this method.

Assignment Number 41

Growing Potatoes

P New potatoes grow from seeds. Seed and new potatoes all look the same. New potatoes will also grow from parts of the old ones provided that there is a shoot or 'eye'.

C You can have a look at a potato and then use part of one to watch the growth.

You will need
Potato, small dish or saucer, a knife, iodine, large flower pot, potting compost (or soil), notebook.

Do this
The potato is called a tuber and contains stored food. Look at it.

You should be able to find

(a) tiny buds. These are situated at the top of small ridges. These are called the eyes. If you look again you should be able to find that most of the eyes are at the top end of the shoot. Some people call this the rose end.

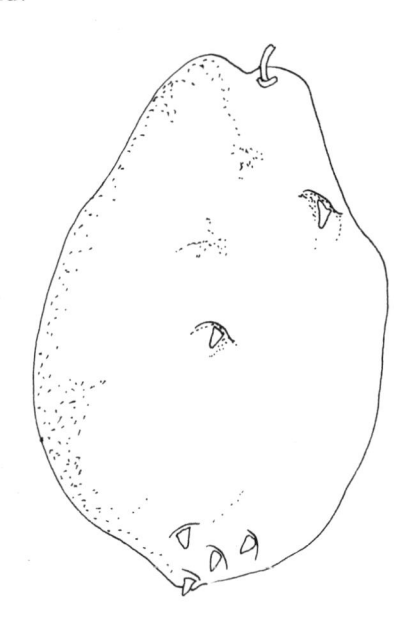

(b) you should also be able to find the place where the stalk from the potato was attached to the parent plant.

Growing the potato
1 Put some damp potting compost in the plant pot — about ¼ full.
2 Cut the potato in half.
3 Weigh the half of potato with the rose.
4 Use the rose end. Place this in the damp compost. Make sure that the uncut side is uppermost. Cover the potato with potting compost to about half way up the pot.

5 Put the pot in a sunny window if possible.
6 Keep an illustrated diary of events. You could have a large sheet on a wall, in your study area.

Date	Notes
26/1/82	Potato planted
7/2/82	First shoots
etc	

7 Make sure the compost remains damp, but do not over-water.
8 Once the shoots come through put more compost over the potato.
9 Leaves should eventually appear.
10 See how long you can manage to grow the potato.
11 Eventually dig it up. Turn the pot upside down on to some paper. You may have some small potatoes.
12 Weigh the potato.
13 Compare weights before and after your investigation.

Think about this
How have the new potatoes developed from the original one?

Primary 3 and 4
We eat potatoes because they contain stored food.

Do this
1 Place the other half of the cut potato (or cut another one in half) onto a plate. Pour a few drops of iodine onto the cut surface.
2 You will see a dark blue/black staining.
3 Starch always turns blue when iodine is added.
4 Take a small amount of household starch and repeat instruction No. 1. Notice the result.
5 If you look around the edge of the potato which you put starch on, you will see that there is a yellow colour under the outer skin. This shows that protein is in this particular area.

Think about this
1 How important are potatoes in the everyday diet of the western world? Compare this with rice and other crops in other parts of the world.
2 Try to discover how the potato reached the western world.

Assignment Number 42

Growing Plants from Cuttings

P Not all plants grow from seeds, and it is a good idea to show children that you can grow them from various parts of plants. This does not work with all species. We suggest some ideas here. You could try them with various common plants which you have.

C Have you ever wondered whether plants only grow from seeds, bulbs and corms. You can try to find out whether other parts of the plant can be made to grow into a new plant.

You will need
Notebook, pencil, plastic bags, moss, some sandy soil, grafting tape (or sellotape is an alternative), a small sharp knife, hormone powder — if it is available, coarse sand, peat, garden soil, 'pots'.

Cuttings
Do this
1 Make up some soil for your cuttings. You will need:

   3 parts of coarse sand
   2 parts of peat
   1 part of garden soil

2 Cut a shoot from a suitable plant like a geranium.

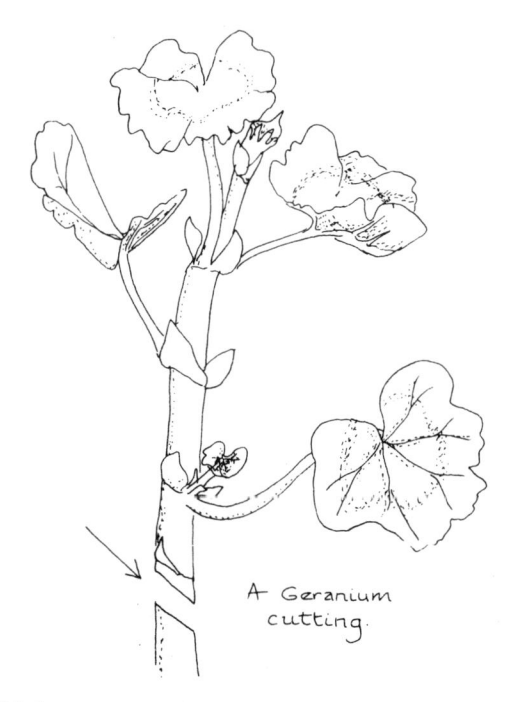

A Geranium cutting.

3 Make sure you do this near a joint.
4 Pull off the lower leaves.
5 Bury the cutting for about half its length in your 'cutting' mixture.
6 Put a plastic bag over the pot.
7 Roots should soon grow.
8 Remove the bag.
9 If you have any hormone rooting powder, you could try using this on one cutting, to see whether it speeds up root formation.

Grafting
You will find that one of the easiest plants to graft is the cactus.

1 You will need two cactus plants. Cut the top off one. This is called the stock.

2 Cut a shoot from the other one. Make sure it fits onto the top of the stock.

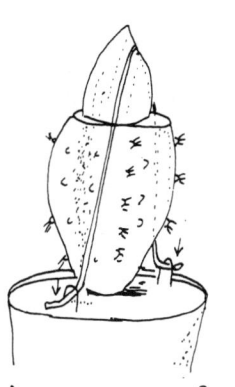

A cactus graft.

3 Hold this in position with a piece of string, which is pushed into the soil by attaching it with small pieces of wire, or even hairgrips.
4 Keep careful records of what you discover.

42 a

Assignment Number 42

Layering
Some plants, like carnations and pinks, grow easily when layering is used.

1 **Partly cut** the shoot from a carnation or pink, at a joint — see the drawing to help you.

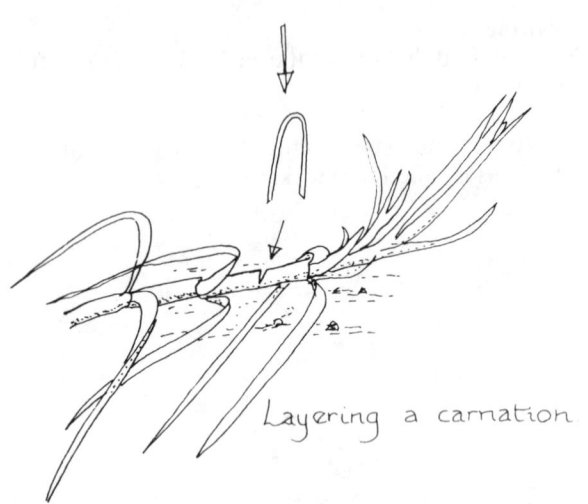

Layering a carnation

2 Peg this down, using a hair grip, or a piece of bent wire.

3 Keep careful records to discover what happens.

Growing new plants from leaves
It is possible to grow new plants from leaves. Although it does not work with many species, you could try it. A good plant to use is the African violet. Begonia will also grow from leaves.

1 If you are using an African violet, carefully remove a leaf, and put it into a pot with some soil in it. You could dip the stalk part of the leaf into hormone rooting powder first.

2 Take off a leaf from a begonia plant.

3 Use hairgrips to peg it down with the veins uppermost.

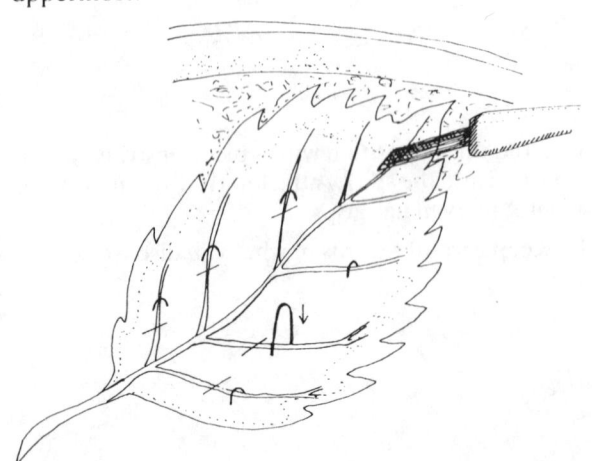

4 Carefully make some small cuts in the veins using a sharp knife.

Think about this
1 How successful were you with your various cuttings?

2 Do you think it is better to grow plants this way or from seeds?

3 Why do you think seeds might also be necessary?

Assignment Number 43

Spores are Invisible

P Children may notice that things go bad. If they do not notice, you can bring it to their attention. Although we can see it happening, we cannot see what causes it. Spores in the air are responsible. They are very tiny. However, by growing the spores of mould we can see what happens when they are allowed to develop. We can do this by setting up a mould garden.

C Have you ever wondered why things sometimes go bad? There are very tiny organisms in the air all the time. These are the spores of minute organisms such as moulds. Although they are so tiny that we cannot see them, we can see what happens when we provide food for them.

You will need
2 jam jars, two dishes/saucers to stand them on, some dry stale bread (preferably brown), water, magnifying glass/hand lens, labels, notebook, pencil.

Do this
1 Cut two pieces of bread to fit under the jam jars.

2 Place one piece of dry bread on one of the saucers.

3 Cover this with one of the jars.

4 This is the control. Mark a label with the letter A and stick it on the jar.

5 Place another piece of dry bread on the second saucer.

6 Moisten the bread with water.

7 Cover the bread with a jam jar.

8 Label this B.

9 Record the details in your notebook. You could use a table like the one below:

Date	A (control)	B
1/2/82	Investigation set up	

10 Look at both pieces of bread regularly using the hand lens. DO NOT take off the jars.

11 Record your information in your notebook.

12 See how long growth continues.

Think about this
1 Did anything grow on A?

2 Did anything grow on B?

3 If anything grew, did it eventually die?

4 If it did, do you think you can explain it?

5 What did you need to do to encourage your mould to grow?

Find out more
1 Why do you think we get colds?

2 Can you find out how other spores are useful?

3 Can you discover something about useful plants which grow from spores?

4 Why do you think moulds do not grow all the while?

5 Find out something about penicillin and how it was 'discovered'.

6 Look up the uses of other moulds.

Growth in Twigs

P All living things grow. The rate at which they do varies from species to species. Parts of living things, like the twigs on trees, can be studied, because they grow. But we seldom know how much twigs grow. We probably also know very little about how slowly or quickly this growth occurs. In some parts of the world growth is more or less regular: in other places it takes place in bursts. In some areas there may be times when growth stops.

By keeping careful records of the growth of twigs through a year it is possible to discover growth patterns.

C Living things are all around us. We probably notice that changes take place when they grow. Twigs are quite easy to measure. By doing this regularly over a period of time we can find out how much they grow. We will need to keep careful records. Choose a tree which is along your walk. This investigation covers a long period. It is important that records are kept regularly and carefully.

You will need
Tree, waterproof felt tip marker (fine point), centimetre ruler, notebook, pencil.

Do this
1 Choose a tree after all the leaves have fallen from it.

2 Select two twigs on the tree. Look at the illustration.

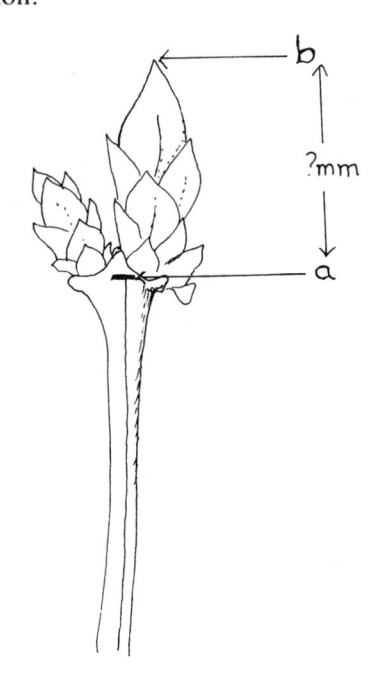

3 Make a small mark just below the bud. Do this with a waterproof marker. You will then be able to recognise your twigs each time you visit the tree.

4 The twig must be measured carefully each week. You will need to take your measurements at a-b as shown in the illustration.

5 Keep a record of your measurements like this.

Date	Length a-b	Observations Changes in twigs.

6 Keep a note of any visible changes which you notice in the twig. For example, its colour, the size of the bud, and so on. Keep these records for at least six months.

Think about this
1 Did you notice any changes in the twig during the time you were keeping records? If you did, can you describe the changes?

2 Are there any times when you have not been able to see any changes?

3 If there are periods when changes are not taking place, can you suggest any reasons for this?

4 Look at your records. Did both twigs grow at the same rate?

Assignment Number 45

Make a Sponge Garden

P & C You can make a living garden using an ordinary sponge. Because the sponge holds water, it will provide enough for plants to begin to grow. You can see how successful you are at growing a sponge garden.

You will need
Natural or plastic sponge (round one if possible), thread, seeds (cress, grass or mustard are suitable), notebook, pencil.

Do this
1 Thread some thread through the sponge. Knot it at one end, so that it will not pull through.
2 Soak the sponge in water.
3 Squeeze it out.

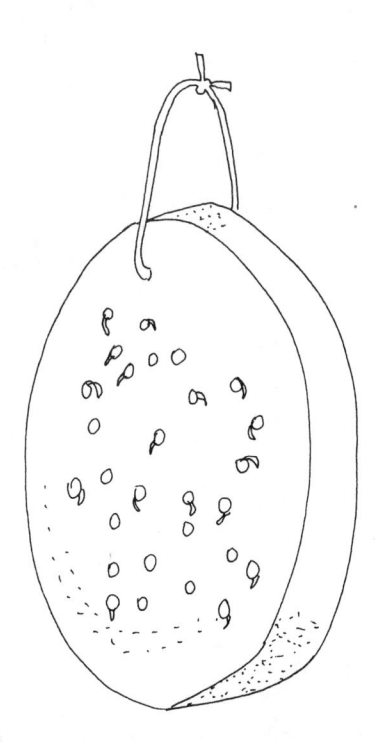

Think about this
1 When the seeds started to germinate could you see where the roots went?
2 Could you see what the roots were like?
3 Could you see where the shoots went?
4 Keep your garden going to see what eventually happens.
5 Do you think your seeds need anything besides water to grow fully?

4 Sprinkle some seeds over the sponge. Grass seeds grow quite quickly once they get damp: cress does not take long to germinate.

5 Alternatively, you could count out a given number — say 50 or 100. You would then be able to see whether they will all germinate.

6 Hang your sponge garden up somewhere, where light from a window will get at it.

7 Keep careful records — when you 'planted' your garden, when the first seeds grew, etc.

45 a

Assignment Number 46

Looking at Life in Water

P Water fascinates children and we will need to try and look at some of the animals which live there. In this way we shall be able to compare and contrast them, and to make comparisons with those animals which we have found living on land.

We should be able to discover something about the problems terrestrial and aquatic animals face. We can pose a number of questions, so that children can investigate the creatures more closely. Primary 3 and 4 will be able to do some sorting. Primary 5 and 6 will be able to take this a step further and actually identify some of their organisms.

Nets can be purchased, but they are expensive. We suggest ways in which simple nets can be made.

Before you start out on your 'water studies' check that the area where you want to work is safe.

C There are many types of animals living in water. We can look at some of these animals. In doing this we should be able to build up a picture of them. We may discover ways in which they feed, move and so on.

Making nets
You can make nets from a variety of materials. If you plan to use your net regularly it is worth sparing a little time on it. Simple fishing nets can be bought cheaply in many toy shops (especially along coastal areas). Others can be made from nylon stockings and tights. But these do not last for very long. A good strong one, can be made from terylene curtain net. Galvanised wire is suitable for making a strong frame. Broom handles or dowel will make good handles.

Follow these step-by-step instructions, referring to the diagrams.

Do this
1 Cut a piece of terylene netting about 25 x 60 cm. Water creatures tend to get trapped in the corners of square net bags, so round off the corners (fig 1).

2 Sew up the bag. The dotted line shows where to sew. Leave a gap of around 5 cm at the top of this (see fig 2).

3 Fold this over the make a hem 2.5 cm deep all the way round. Push the wire through the hem. Do not forget to fasten off your stitching, otherwise your net may come apart at a very important moment.

4 Make a wire frame, using the pliers (fig 3).

5 Bind the wire frame round the dowel to secure the net to the handle (fig 4).

6 If you cannot make one of these nets, you could use a large strong plastic sieve. Attach this to a dowel handle, with strong string by binding it round and round the sieve handle and the wood.

Looking for animals
You will need
Pie dishes, ice cream or margarine containers, plastic spoons, magnifying glass, nature viewer, screw-topped jars, notebook, pencil, recording board, paste jar or pill bottles for individual creatures, aquarium.

46a

Assignment Number 46

Primary 3 and 4
Do this
1 Make some notes about your area of water.
   Is it a pond or a stream?
   Does the water flow slowly or quickly?
   Are there any trees?
   Did you notice any birds on the water?
   Did you notice any signs of animal activity — were there holes, for example?

2 Put some clean water in your dish.

3 We can collect in a number of areas. We must do this carefully, so that we can collect as many of the animals as possible.
   Skim the surface of the water
   Skim through the middle level
   Drag the net along the bottom
   Look under submerged objects, like stones
   Look at the weeds and try to discover whether there are creatures living there
   If there are large objects in the water, like a fallen tree or large rock, carefully investigate these.

4 Dip carefully, trying not to disturb the water too much. Sweep gently against the current.

5 Tip your animals into the dish.

6 Try to discover what you have, and place single specimens in a screw-top jar, with water. You will be able to take these home for further study.

7 Try and record in your notebook whereabouts you found your animals. The simple chart below will help you:

	Mud	gravel	open water	plants in water
Small beetle				
Large beetle				
Mayfly larva				
Small red worm				
Flatworm				
Animal A				
Caddis larva				
Animal B				

You will see that we have 'Animal A' and 'Animal B'. This is because we could not identify them while we were at the stream. Put these in small pots with water, and you will be able to look at them later and try to decide what they are. Label the pots as in the table — 'Animal A', 'Animal B', etc.

8 Take only one specimen of each creature back with you. Can you think of a reason why you should only take one?

9 Take some of the water with you in your screw top jars.

10 When you get home set up an aquarium. See Assignment sheet 47.

You should be able to answer some of the following questions by studying your water creatures carefully. If you cannot see them too easily in the larger aquarium you could place them in smaller glass containers for a short while. A basin or beaker will be suitable. You could also use a nature viewer. Since this does not hold a great deal of water, make sure they only stay here a short while.

Can you see how the creatures move?
Can you discover what they feed on?

If you are keeping your animals for some time, make sure that you know what they feed on; and keep them fed.

Primary 5 and 6
1 When you visit the water habitat for the first time, you could make a simple sketch of your area. We have produced a simple one to show you. Mark on it all the important things — trees, large stones, areas of weed, etc.

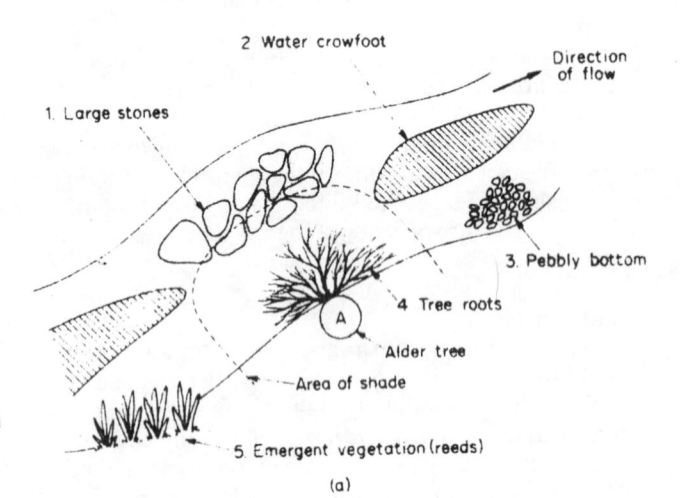

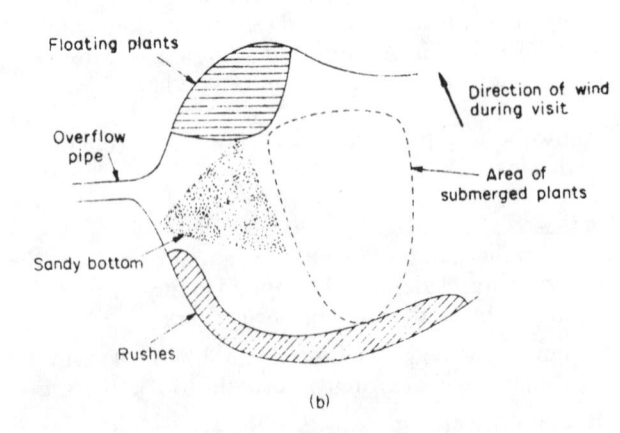

2 When you collect creatures, try to discover something about the population. Are there more of one species than of others? Can you think of some system for grouping the creatures according to the numbers you find? You might be able to count some of them. In other cases there may be so many that counting is impossible.

Don't forget to keep records of your creatures, so that you can perhaps compare results for (a) various areas in your habitat and (b) different aquatic habitats. Take some of your creatures back.

3   Study and compare their movement to discover as much as possible about the way they breathe. Do some come to the surface? If they do, what do they come for? How often do they come?

Look at a fish
Do this
1   Obtain a larger fish from the fishmonger's if possible. (You could use frozen fish instead.) Look at it.

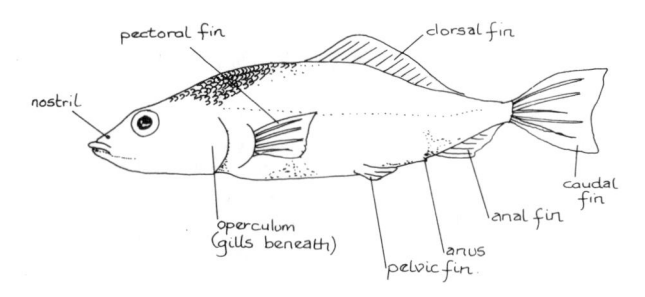

2   Look at its shape and draw it.

3   Look at the fins. Where are they positioned?

4   Look at the fish's gills. Then try the following. Cut a number of plain pieces of tissue paper to size 8 cm x 8 cm. Fasten them together with a small bulldog clip. Hold the clip, and lower the paper into a bowl of water. Wave the clip gently about.
   What do you notice happening?
   Take this out of the water
   What do you notice now?
   Can you see any connection between this and the gills on the fish you have been looking at?

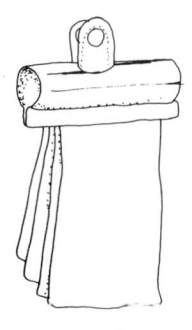

5   Look at the animals in your aquarium, and try and discover what they feed on.

Try and discover what the creatures feed on in their natural state. Make a drawing of a pond or stream. Cut out pictures of various creatures and stick them on. Use only the creatures which you know live in your habitat. Try and draw lines to link the creatures together when you know what they feed on. In this way you will draw up a simple food web, which is made up of food chains.

Assignment Number 47

Setting up an Aquarium

P & C One way of studying our water animals over a longer period of time is to set up an aquarium in which we can keep them. If the instructions given here are followed a successful effort should result.

You will need
An aquarium, gravel, sand, water weeds, water animals, water from the area being studied, sheet of cork (or thin card), aerator pump, notebook, pencil.

Do this
The size and type of aquarium which you intend to use will depend on what you intend to study. If you are only keeping your animals for a short time, it is not really necessary to set up an elaborate aquarium. If you want to keep some animals away from other animals, then you may want a number of small aquaria, rather than one large one. If you want to discover something about what goes on in the pond or stream, then you may decide that you want a larger aquarium for keeping all your creatures together.

1 Make sure that the tank is clean.

2 Do not use soap powders or detergents for cleaning the tank. Even small traces could kill the animals.

3 Wash the gravel.

4 Put about 3 cm of gravel in the bottom of the tank.

5 Add the plants, ensuring that they are firmly anchored by tieing them around stones.

6 Fill the tank with water — preferably using that which you have brought back with you — if this was possible. If not, take some water from the tap, but leave it to stand for a few days.

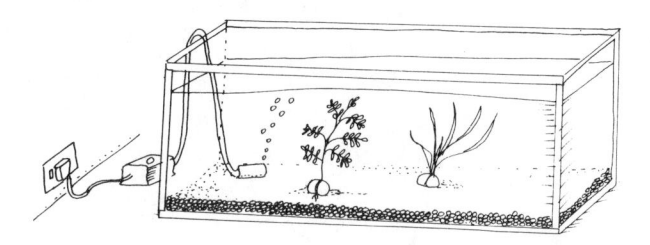

7 Place a sheet of cork (or card) on the gravel, and carefully pour your water onto this. This will prevent the gravel from being disturbed. Remove it as soon as the tank is full.

8 When you have set up you aquarium, leave it for a few days, before introducing your animals.

9 You can use the creatures for various studies as suggested in other Assignments.

Simple short term alternative pond.
1 Cut down a cardboard box so that it has 5cm sides. Line the inside with polythene, so that it hangs over the edge.

2 Put in some water.

3 Introduce your animals and plants.

4 Do not use this for too long. Use an aerator pump all the while so that any animals have a sufficient supply of oxygen.

47 a

Assignment Number 48

Making Tracks

P & C However much we watch our wild creatures round about us, we are only going to find out a little about them directly. Animals are secretive, but there is one way of finding out some of the things which go on whilst we are not about.

One way of doing this is by tracking animals. This will help to fill in missing information from our picture. This is an activity which can be started by Primary 3 and 4 and actively pursued by Primary 5 and 6, since the older children will be able to make more deductions than the younger ones.

You will need
Notebook, pencil, plaster making equipment (see Assignment sheet 49).

Do this
Trees
1. Take a good look at trees:

    (a) Can you see any signs that animals have attacked the bark?

    (b) Can you see any signs which tell you that certain animals live there?
    There might be larger animals, like squirrels (with their dreys (homes) in the branches), or smaller ones, like spiders (you might find their webs).

Burrows
Look for holes which might belong to various animals. If you find any, look at them very carefully. The size will give you a clue as to the size of the animal which has been there.

Carefully investigate where the holes are, what their shape is, whether there is more than one, and so on. Look for signs that animals have been about. What activity can you see? You might find soil thrown out, you could find old bedding, you might find the remains of food outside.

Animal remains
You are likely to come across animal remains from time to time. You might find feathers or skeletons. It is possible that the animal might have died naturally, perhaps from an illness or old age. Put on a pair of rubber gloves before you investigate carcasses, because they might be carrying disease.

Look around you for feathers. When you have found some examine them carefully. A feather here and there probably means that a bird is moulting. However, if you find blood, and other remains of birds, you might suspect that it has been killed by another animal. See if you can discover what might have killed it. Try to look for signs of the direction in which the culprit went. In snowy weather, this is often easier, as you can usually find tracks. You might also discover other signs — perhaps of a struggle at this time of the year. You can perhaps see wing marks in the snow, or other signs that the animals have been in combat. Soft mud also gives us a number of clues.

Leaves of trees
Take a careful look at the leaves on trees. Can you discover any which have been attacked in any way? Are there some, which have been eaten or torn? You may actually discover some of the animals on the trees.

Food hordes
You might discover collections of unused or used food. Nuts and berries are collected by many different animals. Try looking further to see if you can discover which creatures have been responsible for collecting them together.

There may be other clues close by. Perhaps there are burrows, homes (like dreys and nests), and so on. This does not necessarily mean that they belong to these animals, but it is perhaps narrowing it down. You need to be a careful detective. You will have to piece together the various clues which you find, until you are certain that you have a good 'case'.

Animal droppings
This might not seem a very interesting area for discovery. But animal droppings give us a clue as to the animals which might have been about. Do not touch the droppings unless you have rubber gloves. You might find collections of animal droppings in some instances. This might suggest that animals collect together in certain areas. This is true of rabbits, for example. Badgers are very clean animals and use latrines (toilets) for their droppings.

Pellets
Some birds, like owls, get rid of the remains of their food which they cannot eat. You will usually find some pellets under owl roosts. By collecting these you you will be able to find out what food the creature has eaten. Take them home and take them apart.

Footprints
Both mammals and birds will leave their footprints in both soft mud and snow. You can make plaster casts of these footprints. Details for making these will be found on Assignment sheet 49.

You will need
A strip of card about 5 cm deep, paper clips, newspaper and for prints in snow, hairspray.

48 a

Assignment Number 48

Do this
1 Place the card around the footprint to form a collar.

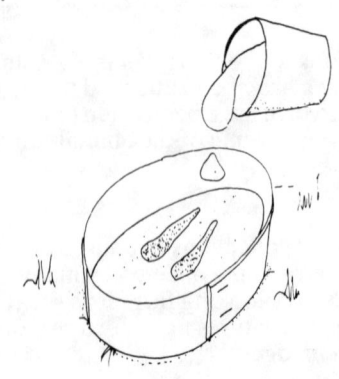

2 Fasten the ends with a paper clip: thus forming a circle.
3 In snow, first spray the footprint with hairspray.
4 Make up the plaster as directed.
5 In snow, use melted snow, or very cold water to mix the plaster.
6 When the plaster has set, use a trowel to lift up the print.

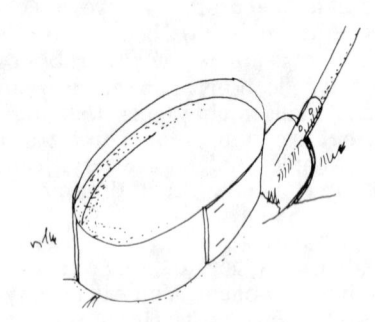

7 Wrap it in newspaper. Take it back.

8 Clean it under running water, using an old toothbrush.
9 Make a collection of prints. Make sure you find out what they were made by. You can paint them to make them stand out from the background.

Assignment Number 49

Plaster Casting

P & C Plaster casting is a simple way of keeping records of bark patterns, animal movements (tracks), etc. This assignment sheet suggests how to make plaster casts. There are references in the various sheets (e.g. tracking) as to where this method can be employed. You might discover other places where you can plaster cast, and you can use the technique which is described here to help you.

You will need
Plaster of paris, mixing containers (yoghurt cups, plastic cups, etc are useful, as they are disposable), stirrers (e.g. wooden lollipop stick or spoon), dry spoon, water, screw top bottle.

NB It is difficult to tell you how much plaster you will need, because moulds vary in size. You will soon get used to how much to use.

Do this
1   Put some water in the mixing containers (about 1/8 of the depth). You should always add plaster to water, and NOT water to plaster.

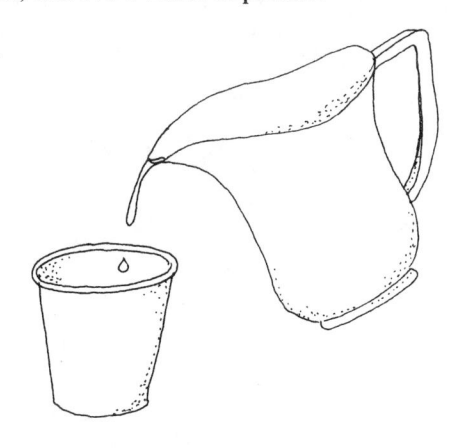

2   Use a dry spoon and add plaster to the water.

3   Stir carefully, ensuring, as far as you can, that bubbles are not allowed to get in.

4   Continue adding plaster until you have a mixture which is like 'thick cream'.

5   The plaster is now ready to pour into any mould which you have made (see Assignment sheet 27). Tap the side of the container so that you get rid of the air bubbles.

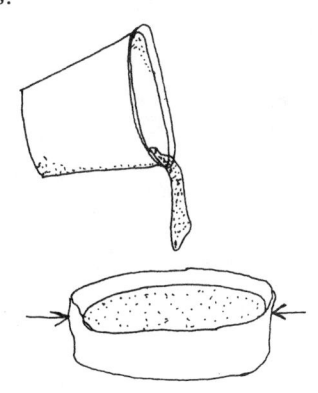

6   If you make the plaster too thin, it takes a long while to set, and tends to be weak. If it is too thick, it is difficult to pour, and does not spread evenly onto the mould.
Practice makes perfect — usually!

7   Remember to wash your equipment immediately after use. If you do not, the plaster sets and is difficult to remove.

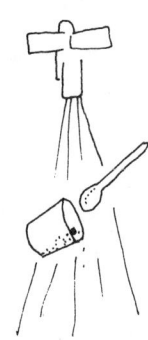

8   After about an hour if the plaster seems firm peel away the mould and allow the plaster to dry for 24 hours.

49 a

Assignment Number 50

Looking at Cells

P All living things, both plants and animals, are made of cells. The cells vary in shape and function depending in which part of a plant or animal they are found. By looking at the cells in a moss leaf and from an animal, it is possible to make simple comparisons between plant and animal life.

C Have you ever wondered what you are made of? Not sugar and spice and all things nice, like the rhyme, but cells. We can look at some of these to see what they are like.

You will need
Moss plant, forceps (or fine knitting needle), notebook, pencil, microscope, water, microscope slide, cover slip, straw, dropping pipette, hand lens, windpipe (trachea) from either a pig or sheep (obtainable from a butcher or abattoir).

Do this
1 Look at the back of your hand with the magnifying glass or hand lens.
2 Describe what you can see and make a drawing.
3 Use a straw to scrape the inside of the windpipe (trachea) of the pig or sheep.
4 You should have a drop of liquid on the end of your straw — unless the trachea happens to be old. In this case put a drop of water on the slide.

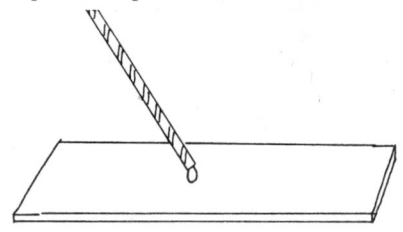

5 If you gently touch the microscope slide with the straw, some of the cells will be left there.

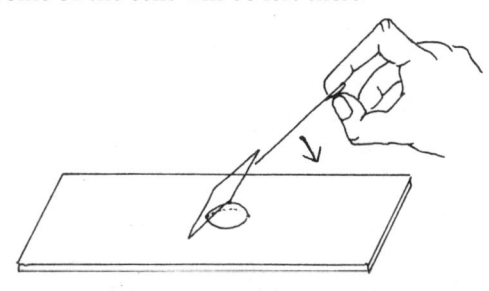

6 Carefully lower the cover slip on top of this. Use your forceps to do this — or a fine knitting needle.

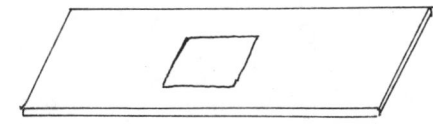

7 Try to make sure that you do not trap any air bubbles.
8 Put your slide under the microscope and look at it carefully.

9 You will probably find that even if you were very careful when you lowered the cover slip, you still have air bubbles. These show up as quite large circles, the edges of which are dark in colour.
10 If you look more closely you should see some of the cells.
11 See if you can draw them without looking at the illustration — don't cheat now!
12 Once you have completed your drawing you can compare it with the illustration. You can now make another slide using the moss plant.

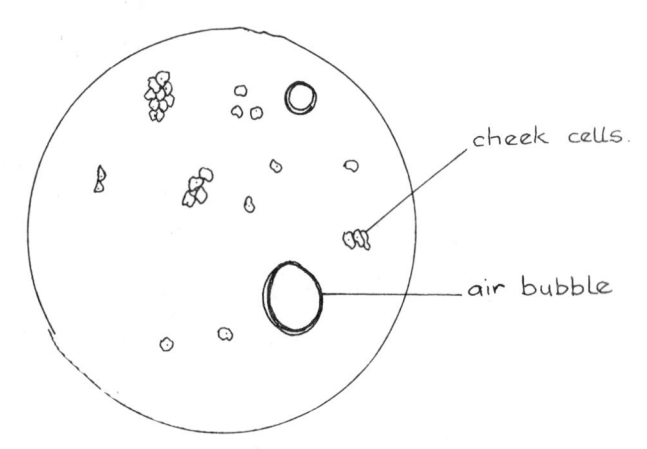

13 Take off an inmost leaf from the shoot of the moss plant. You will find it easier if you use your forceps to do this.
14 Use your dropping pipette to place one drop of water on a clean microscope slide.
15 Use your forceps to put the leaf into the drop of water.
16 Carefully lower the cover slip onto the slide. Try to make sure that you do not trap air bubbles.
17 Place the slide under the microscope.
18 Look very carefully.
19 Make careful drawings of what you can see.

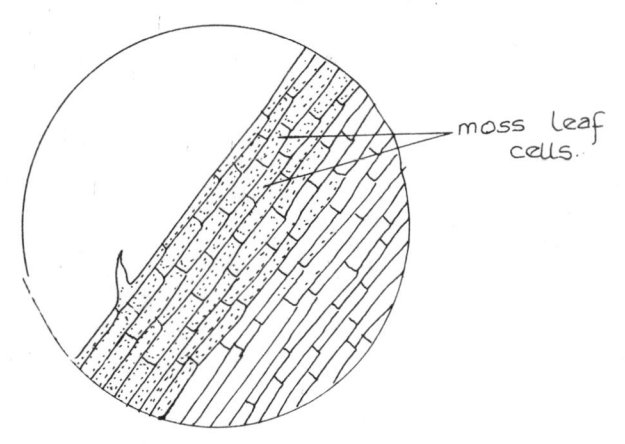

20 You can use the skin from any green plants.

50a

Assignment Number 50

Thinking about this
1 You should be able to see that the moss leaf has divisions. These are the cells.

2 See if you can see green areas inside the moss cells. These are called chloroplasts. What shape are they? Did you see these in the animal cells from the trachea?
These chloroplasts contain a green colouring (pigment) called chlorophyll, which gives the leaf its colour.

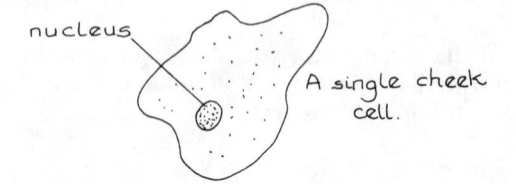

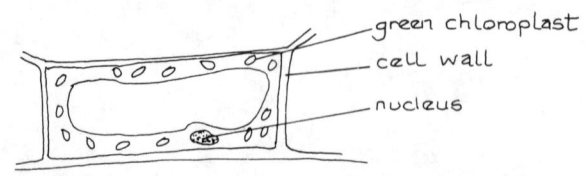

nucleus — A single cheek cell.

green chloroplast
cell wall
nucleus

A single moss leaf cell.

Assignment Number 51

Looking at Frameworks

When we look at most living things, we find that they have some kind of framework. A tree has one; most kinds of animals have them. We can look at framework skeletons.

You will need
Pipe cleaners, small cloth bag or piece of cloth, animal skeletons (if possible), pictures of different animals — birds, mammals, fish, reptiles, amphibians and invertebrates, like beetles.

Do this
1 Try to pull the cloth or cloth bag into a shape. You will find that it doesn't stay where it is for very long.

2 Now make a skeleton (framework) using the pipe cleaners, and place this under the bag or cloth. What differences did you notice?

3 Get your children to discuss and talk about the frameworks in non-living things — buildings, cars, bridges, etc.

4 If you have discovered a skeleton or part of one on your walks you will be able to use this.

5 If not, look at the animal pictures. See if you can find pictures of very large beetles to compare in size with even the smallest mammals.

Think about this
1 Why do you think there are no very large insects?

2 Where do invertebrates (animals without backbone) have their skeletons?

3 Do you think this has anything to do with their small size?

Primary 5 and 6
Do this
1 Draw your own skeleton.

2 Look at the X-ray photograph on this sheet. You will be able to see the bones underneath the flesh.

Think about this
1 Why is it a good idea for motor cyclists to wear crash helmets?

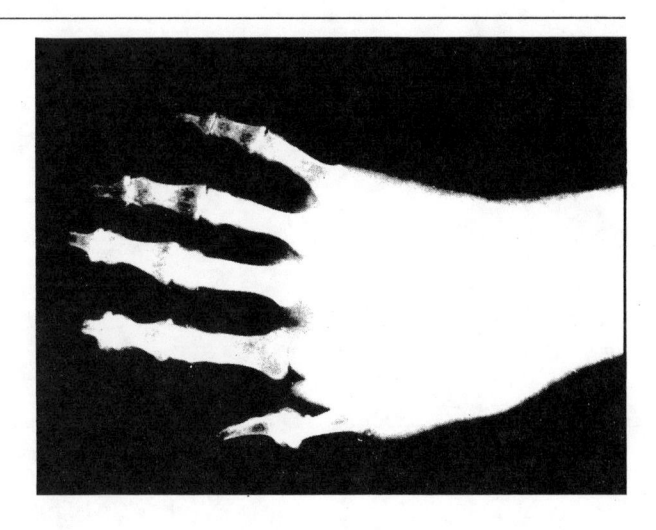

Assignment Number 52

Tongue Rolling and Tongue Folding

P There is one characteristic which is passed from parent to child, and this is the ability to roll the tongue and fold the tongue. You can make a check against parents and offspring to see whether they can do this.

C We get lots of characteristics from our parents. We can see the colour of our eyes, and compare them with our parents. We also inherit other things. One of these is the ability to roll our tongues and fold our tongues.

You will need
Notebook, pencil, mirror.

Do this
1 Test each member of the family
 (a) to see whether they can roll their tongue and

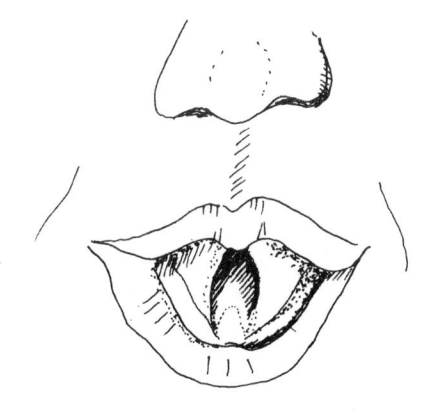

(b) fold their tongue.

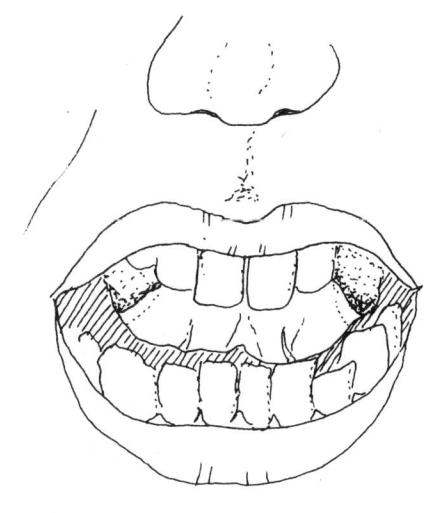

Think about this
1 If you can roll and fold your tongue, then it is likely that your parents can.

2 If you cannot do this then your parents might not be able to either.

Assignment Number 53

Heights and Weights

P & C We can keep careful records of the way in which we grow as a regular activity, and plot this information as graphs. By keeping careful, regular records we will be able to discover whether heights and weights show regular increases.

You will need
Long piece of paper or several pieces joined together to form your height chart, pen, notebook, scales, ruler, tape.

1 Make a height measurement chart. You could decorate it with things you have seen on your walk.

2 Mount this on the door or the wall of your workroom or bedroom.

3 Take regular measurements.

4 Ask all the family to do it.

5 Record your heights on your chart.

6 Weigh yourself regularly.

7 Ask all the family to weigh themselves at the same time.

8 Keep these measurements in your small notebook.

Think about this
1 After a time plot these measurements on graphs.

2 Look closely at these to see how people grow.

3 See if you can discover whether we grow regularly.

4 See whether we put on the same amount of weight regularly.

5 Do adults grow?

6 Does their weight change?

53 a

Assignment Number 54

How Quickly do we React?

P We all react differently in different situations. If a kettle is boiling on the stove we will turn it off. If, however, we see a young child moving towards the kettle, then we are likely to react even more quickly. Similarly, if we see a child about to step into a road when a car is coming we would take the necessary action.

We can test how quickly we react. We can also discover whether our reaction times improve with practice. Playing games soon speeds up (most!) people's reaction times.

In this simple investigation, we see how quick various people's reactions are, and then see whether practice improves them.

C You know how quickly you move when you see something unexpected coming towards you. Sometimes you might be sucessful at moving away from a ball which someone is throwing. Sometimes you might want to catch that ball, and so you react. How quick you are will depend on how easy it is to catch the ball. If you play games, like cricket or hockey, you will soon realise that the more you practice, the better you become because you react more quickly. We can see how quickly we react with a simple investigation, and whether our reaction improves with practice. You might also like to test other people's reactions.

You will need
30 cm ruler, notebook, pencil.

Do this
1 You will need to work in pairs for this investigation.

2 One person holds the ruler as shown in the illustration. The 'O' should be at the bottom. The subject does not touch the ruler, but has to make sure that once it is released it will fall into his/her hand.

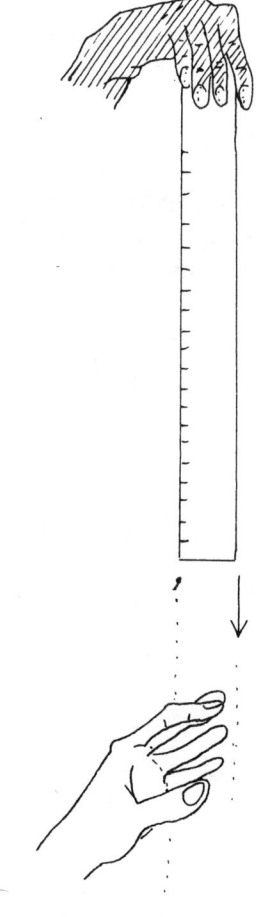

3 The partner drops the ruler without telling the subject when he is going to let go.

4 As the ruler is dropped the subject has to catch it as quickly as possible.

5 Record the result. The lower the reading — e.g. 10 cm as opposed to 20 cm — the quicker the reaction.

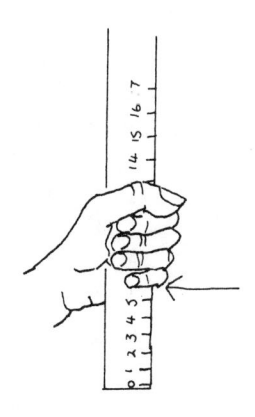

6 Repeat the experiment several times recording each measurement.

54a

Assignment Number 54

Think about this
1 Does the reaction time improve with practice?

Primary 5 and 6
Do this
1 Repeat the investigation with the left and right hands.

Think about this
1 Is our reaction quicker with the hand which we normally use. For example if you write right-handed, was your reaction better with this hand than the left?

2 Make a comparison of various people's reactions taking into account whether they are right or left handed.

Find out more
1 Think of other methods of measuring and investigating reaction times.

Assignment Number 55

How our Arms and Legs Move

P   It is difficult to show in detail how the arms and legs operate. Muscles which move the arms can be felt, and the use of a simple model will help to show how they work.

C   When we went for our walk, we moved our legs, our arms, perhaps we did some drawings. We certainly moved our eyes from side to side, perhaps up and down. We listened to the sounds around us. We could do all these things because we have muscles to move our bones, or parts of our eye, for example. You can feel your muscles, but because they are hidden under our flesh, we cannot see them. However, we can make a simple model to show how they work.

You will need
Strong card, paper fastener, scissors, two small equal sized elastic bands — they must be the same length, thickness, etc. notebook, pencil.

Do this
1   Hold your arm out straight, and feel the muscles of the lower arm and upper arm move.

2   Now bend your arm, and feel what is happening to the muscles.

3   Can you describe what happens.

4   You could repeat the same action with your legs.

5   Make a model arm in two pieces to represent the upper arm, from the shoulder to elbow and the lower arm from elbow to fingertips.

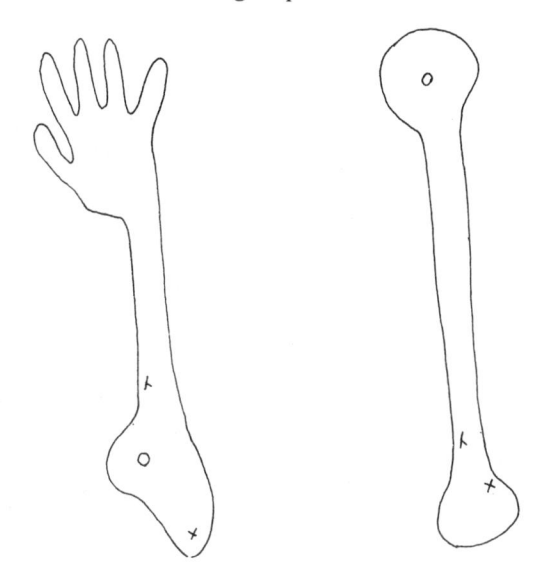

6   Fasten the two pieces together with a fastener. Make sure that they move easily.

7   Staple the elastic bands in the positions shown on the illustration.

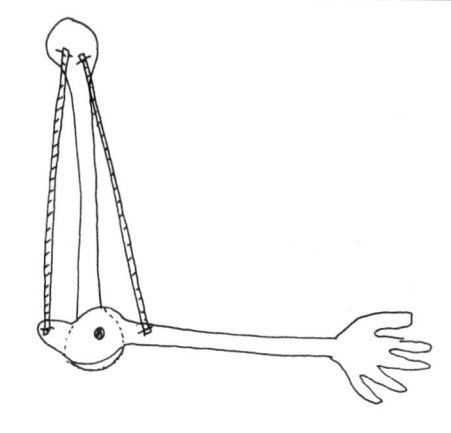

8   Move the lower arm up and down.

9   Watch what happens to the bands.

Think about this
1   Can you see why we need muscles to help us move?

2   Muscles are not the only things which help us move. We can move our arm at the elbow, because we also have joints.

3   Make a list of the places in the body where we have joints.

Find out more
1   Are all our joints the same?

2   How do the different ones work?

3   Can you find out what different names we use for the various joints?

4   Discover whether some joints allow us to move more than others.

5   Find out about smaller animals for example, what sort of joints insects have.

55 a

Assignment Number 56

Listening to Sounds

P We tend to rely on more than one sense at a time in order to get an accurate picture of what is going on around us (See Assignment sheet 75). In this investigation we can reinforce this concept. If we are blindfolded we cannot always tell where a particular sound is coming from.

You will need to carry out a simple investigation to discover what sounds your child can hear. If you use an object which makes too loud a sound they will hear all the while.

C Have you ever wondered how well we can really hear? Do you think that being blindfolded will stop you from discovering which direction a sound is coming from? In this investigation we can find out.

You will need
Notebook, pencil, an object which rattles (bunch of keys, for example), blindfold.

1 Although this can be carried out inside the house, it is better if it is outside where there is a solid piece of ground. The more people there are to take part the more interesting the investigation becomes.

2 The subject is blindfolded, and seated in the centre of a piece of ground.

3 The person with the object moves round slowly, dropping the keys at various points.

4 As soon as the subject hears them drop, he must immediately indicate the place where the sound came from.

5 If you record your results like this you will find out the directions in which the subject has the most accurate hearing.

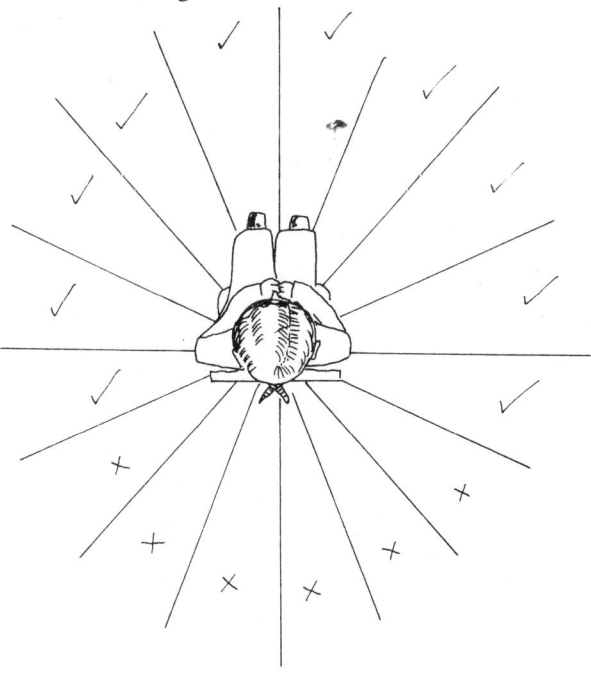

6 If there are a lot of people taking part in the investigation it is better to pass round one bunch of keys quietly, rather than use several different bunches which might make louder (or quieter) noises.

7 A variation on this is to use different objects which the subject has seen before the investigation starts. When they are dropped, not only does he/she have to pinpoint the location, but also try and say what it was which was making the noise.

8 Repeat the investigation with the person not blindfolded, and see whether there are any differences.

Think about this
1 Was it easy to discover where the sound was coming from with the blindfold on?

2 Can you explain why it might have been difficult?

Primary 5 and 6
P & C This is another simple investigation which will help you to discover more about the location of sounds.

You will need
Polythene tubing, 2 plastic funnels, notebook, pencil, blindfold.

Do this
1 Attach some polythene tubing to the stems of the polythene funnels.

2 Place the funnels over your ears.

3 Put on a blindfold.

4 Let someone move the tubes.

5 Listen to sounds.

6 Can you tell where they are coming from?

Think about this
1 If you found it difficult to tell where the sounds were coming from why do you think this was?

Assignment Number 57

Sounds from Hidden Objects

P We cannot always recognise objects from the sounds which they make. For this investigation you will need to place six different familiar objects in six different tins (these tins should be of the same size). Use the same size tins if possible. Do not let the child see the objects.

C A number of objects have been hidden in tins. You will have seen the objects often, because they are common. The idea is to try and discover what they are by listening to the sounds which they make.

You will need
Six tins, notebook, pencil.

Do this
1 Shake each of the six tins in turn.
2 Write down what you think is in them.

Think about this
1 If you found it difficult to decide what was in the tins, why do you think this was?

Assignment Number 58

Hearing Distances

P & C Although we all think we hear the same things, we are all different, and have hearing differences. You can discover whether this statement is true or not, by using a 'ticking' clock or watch.

You will need
Notebook, pencil, clock or watch (with a tick! — not a digital or electronic one), metre rule.

Do this
1 Work in twos.
2 Sit in a quiet room.
3 Move the watch away from someone's ear, along the metre rule.
4 Ask them to tell you when they can no longer hear it. Record the distance.
5 If you think they might be cheating, try it with a blindfold, but do not cover the ears!
6 Try it with both ears.
7 Try it with as many people as possible.

Think about this
1 Did you discover any differences between left and right ears?
2 Did you discover differences between different people?

Further study
See what you can find out about hearing in other animals. Bats use a special type of system — called echo-location. See how much you can discover about this. See if you can find out why one bat doesn't collide with another bat when using this system. □

58a

Assignment Number 59

How are Sounds Caused?

P Sounds are around us all the time, and all are caused by vibrations. Although all sounds are made 'naturally' — being caused by vibrations — we find some more acceptable than others. The sound of music is one of these, and the sound of an aeroplane usually isn't!

These simple investigations will enable the child to discover something about the way sounds are made. Choose two of the experiments for Primary 3 and 4 and the rest for Primary 5 and 6.

C If you stop and listen you will hear all sorts of sounds. Do you know how sounds are made? With these simple investigations, you should be able to discover something about them.

You will need
Balloon, comb, tissue paper, rubber bands, cardboard box, ruler, cotton, 15 cm nails, pencil, notebook, plasticine, elastic, empty bottles of different sizes, water, nails, block of wood, hammer, stick, thin string about 10 m long, tins (e.g. cans with a bottom but no top — and no sharp edges).

Do this
Make your own simple telephone. You will need two people to work your phone.

1. Make holes in the bottom of each of the tins. Use your hammer and nail to do this.
2. Now push the string through the holes and knot it. One end of the string goes through the hole in one tin, and the other end of the string through the hole in the other tin.

3. One person needs to hold one tin; the other person the second tin.
4. Move away from each other until the string is tight. If it has kinks in it, you can dampen it to get rid of these.
5. One person holds the tin to their ear, whilst the second person speaks into the other one.

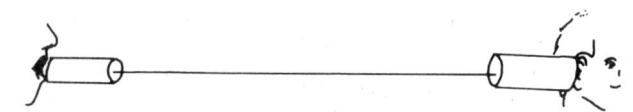

6. Record what happens.
7. Alternate talking and listening.

Think about this
1. Could you hear what the other person was saying?
2. Do you think that if the string were made longer, you could still hear anything? You could try it.

Listening to sounds 'travelling'.
Do this
1. Lie down with one ear close to the ground.
2. Get someone to walk about close by.
3. Get them to move away.
4. Change positions so that each person can discover if anything happens.
5. Record your observations.

Think about this
1. Could you hear anything?
2. If you could what did it sound like?
3. What could you hear and why?
4. Was there a point at which you could not hear anything — when the person who was walking around moved too far away?

Sounds are caused by vibrations
Do this
1. Cover a clean comb with a piece of tissue paper.
2. Hum a tune onto the tissue paper.

Think about this
1. Did you feel anything happening to your lips as you hummed the tune?

Do this
1. Blow up a balloon.
2. Hold this with the tips of your fingers.
3. Place it close to your lips.
4. Make an 'ooh' sound with your lips.

Think about this
1. Did you feel anything happening to the balloon?
2. Can you explain it?

Various things vibrate
To make sounds the vocal chords in your throat vibrate.

Do this
1. Hold your thumb and forefinger very **lightly** against your Adam's apple.
2. Now sing a note or two.

Think about this
1. What did you discover happened?

Do this
1. Push a ruler under a desk lid or into a drawer.
2. Make sure that a part of the ruler sticks out.
3. Twang the ruler.
4. Watch what happens to the ruler.

Think about this
1. What did you see?
2. Did you hear anything?

59a

Assignment Number 59

Do this
1. Stretch an elastic band across a cardboard box.
2. Watch the band carefully.
3. Pluck it with your fingers.

Think about this
1. What did you notice happening?
2. Did you hear anything?

Do this
1. Now pluck the band again.
2. Now hold something like a ruler against the band.
3. Record what you saw.

Do this
1. Attach a length of cotton to a 15 cm nail.
2. Hold the cotton in your fingers, so that the nail is hanging down.
3. Hit the nail gently with your pencil.

Think about this
1. What did you hear?
2. Can you explain how it happened?

Do this
1. Hit the nail again.
2. While it is still making a noise, stop it by holding it with your fingers.

Think about this
1. Did you notice anything when you touched the nail?
2. Why did the sound stop when you touched it?

Do this
1. Hold an elastic band tightly across the top of an empty open tin.
2. Twang the rubber band.

Think about this
1. What did you hear?

Do this
1. Hold an elastic band loosely across the tin.

Think about this
1. What did you hear now?

Do this
1. Use a thick and thin elastic band, and stretch both across the end of a tin.
2. Pluck each band in turn.

Think about this
1. What sort of note does the thin band make?
2. What sort of note does the thick band make?

Do this
1. Make three different weights from plasticine.
2. Hang each one from different length pieces of elastic. Use the same sort of elastic for each.
3. Pluck each of the three bands.

Think about this
1. Record what you hear.
2. Was there a difference in the sounds?
3. If there was, can you explain why?
4. Look at the lengths and thicknesses of the elastic bands.

Do this
1. Put various amounts of water into the same size bottles. Tap them gently with something like a ruler.

Think about this
1. Did you notice anything?

Do this
1. Experiment with these bottles, other bottles, more water, less water, and so on.
2. Do not forget to record your observations.

Do this
1. Take some long nails and knock them into a block of wood, so that they are all at different heights.
2. Hit each nail with your pencil or ruler.
3. Record what you discover.

Think about this
1. Did you get the same or different sounds from your nails?
2. Can you explain why there were differences?

Find out more
1. Make a collection of pictures of as many different musical instruments as you can. Against each write how the sound is produced.
2. Can you find out why bats make some sounds which we cannot hear?
3. Are there other animals which make sounds which we cannot hear?
4. How does the grasshopper make its chirping noise?
5. Can you discover whether there are any other 'musical' insects?

Assignment Number 60

Teeth and Feeding

P & C We can look at our own teeth and compare adult teeth with children's teeth.

You will need
Small mirror (on a handle if possible), clean plasticine, notebook, pencil, plaster of paris, spoon, yoghurt carton (or other disposable container for mixing plaster), water.

Do this
1 Wash your hands.
2 Feel your teeth with your fingers.
3 How many different sorts can you feel?
4 Use the mirror to look at your teeth.
5 Look at someone else's teeth.
6 You can make a cast of your teeth.
7 Shape a piece of clean unused plasticine into a sausage. Form it into a 'U' shape like the illustration.

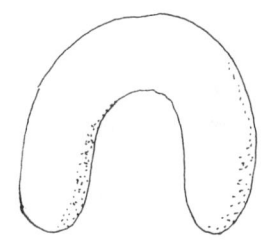

8 Fill in the centre part with more plasticine.

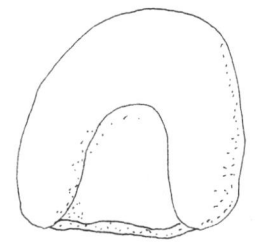

9 Check that there are no fillings or loose teeth in your mouth.

10 Get someone else to put the plasticine into your mouth.

11 Bite on it fairly hard, so that it makes a good impression of both top and bottom teeth. You can bite almost through it.

12 Carefully remove the plasticine from the mouth.

13 The upper set of teeth will be on one side of the plasticine, the lower set on the other.

14 To make a plaster cast roll out a strip of plasticine, flatten it and make a wall round either the top or bottom print.

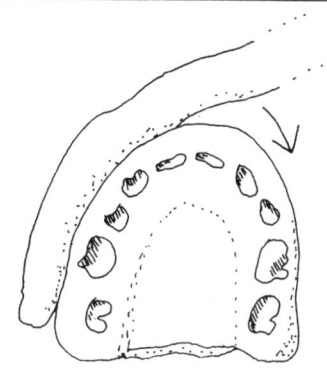

15 Refer to Assignment sheet 49 for details of making up plaster of paris for plaster casting.

16 Pour the plaster into the mould. Make sure it goes into all the holes. Use your spoon or stick to do this.

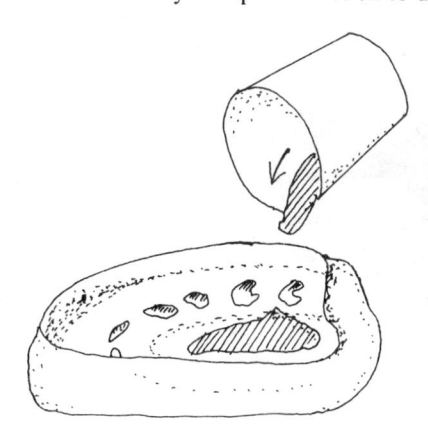

17 Smooth the top.

18 The plaster should set fairly quickly, but leave it for an hour or so to harden.

19 Remove the plasticine carefully.

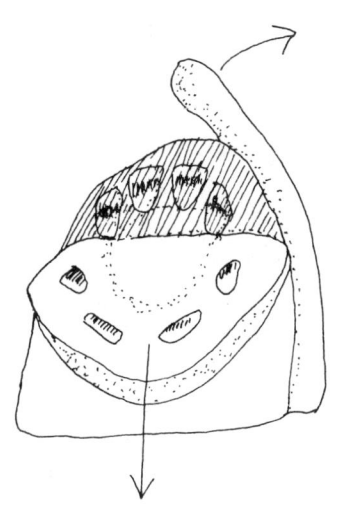

20 You can look at the impression now, but leave the plaster overnight to harden.

60 a

Assignment Number 60

Think about this
1 Look at the different types of teeth.
2 How many different kinds can you find? How many sorts of each do we have?
3 Try and discover what each sort is used for.

Find out more
1 Look at other animals' teeth, and see if they have different kinds. Do their teeth do different jobs? Are there some animals which do not have some of the teeth which we have? Can you explain this?

□

Feeling Hot and Cold

P & C We rely on our senses to tell us what is going on around us. But do our senses always give us an accurate picture? Do the nerve endings on the hand always work 'well?'

You will need
Three containers large enough to put hands in, cold water (from tap), warm water (37°C), hot water (50°C), timer, towel, (don't disclose the temperatures of the water at this stage), thermometer (for checking water temperature), notebook, pencil.

Do this
1 When you are ready to begin the experiment, put cold water in one container, warm water in a second and hot in the third.

2 Arrange the hot and cold containers as in the diagram.

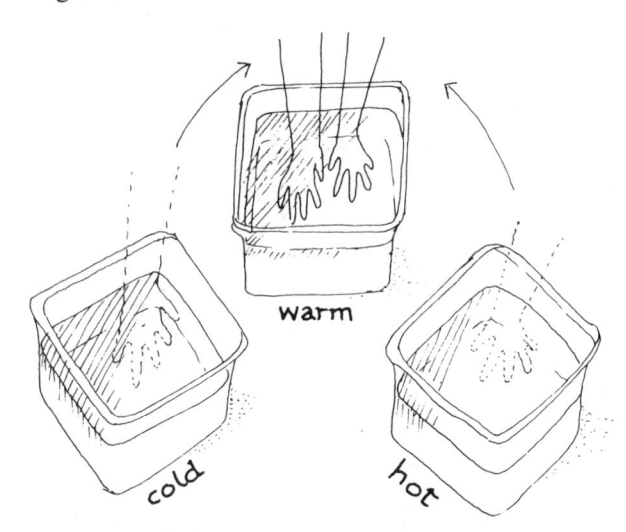

3 The subject places one hand in the cold water and the other in the hot water, without looking.

4 They leave their hands here for one minute.

5 They then plunge both hands into the warm water.

Think about this
1 What do you feel when you put your hands in the warm water?

2 What does your right hand tell you about the temperature of the water?

4 If both your hands are different, why do you think this is?

5 Is it possible that both of our hands are giving our brains the right message?

6 Is it a very good idea to use the senses in our hands to give us information about the temperature of the water?

Assignment Number 62

Finding out about Pain

P & C Our five senses are very important to us. They continually make us aware of what is going on in the environment around us.

Some of the sensations which we receive from our senses are painful; like the sting from a wasp, for example. Although these are painful they are very important to us.

You will need
Fine, non-toxic washable felt tip marker, notebook, pin (or bristle from a brush), blindfold, pencil.

Do this
1 Work in twos.

2 Draw a small square about 3 cm x 3 cm on the back of your hand, using the felt tip marker.

3 Divide the square into 36 smaller ones.

4 Draw the same diagram in your notebook.

5 One person should be blindfolded.

6 Carefully test each of the small squares in turn with the point of the pin (or bristle).

NB It is only necessary to touch the surface very gently with the pin. If using a pin do not pierce the skin. You could use the bristle from a brush instead.

5 The subject needs to tell you when he/she feels pain, and **not** the pressure of the pin.

6 When pain is felt put a 'P' in the identical square in your notebook.

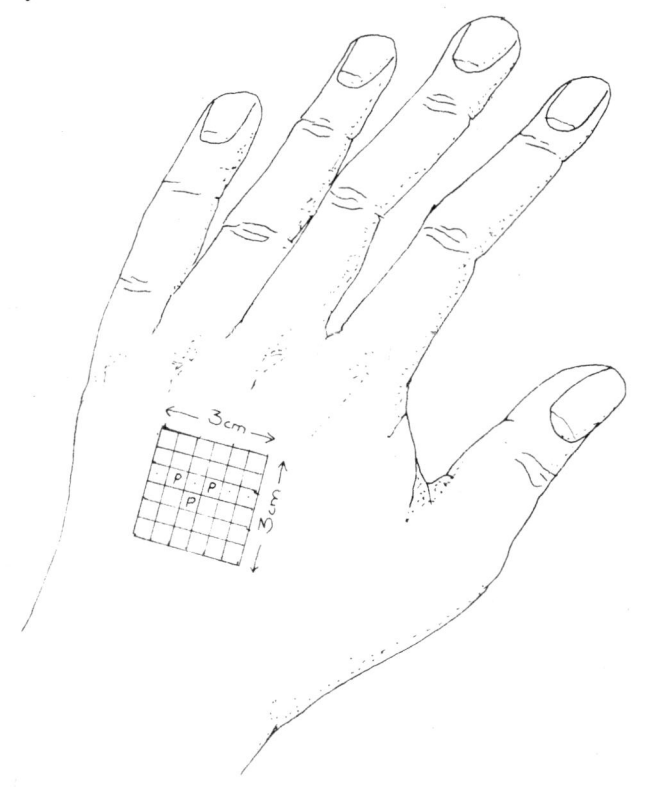

7 Repeat for all the squares.

Think about this
1 Are there 'P's' in all the squares?

2 Why is this?

3 Why we do not need to have nerve endings which detect pain as close together as the pin tests.

4 Why do we need to feel pain — it does hurt!? Can you think of examples when pain is actually very necessary (e.g. when you put your hand on something hot)?

4 Make a list of the times when pain is 'useful'.

62 a

Assignment Number 63

Finding out about Touch

P & C We have already looked closely at one area of the hand to see how close our pain spots are. Now we can find out something more about our sense of feeling in various parts of the body. We can start with the hands.

You will need
Notebook, pencil, feather, blindfold.

Do this
1   Work in twos.

2   Draw round your hands in your notebook. If your hands are too big for your notebook, use a piece of paper. You can fold this and stick it in later. Make sure that you have a back and a front of your hand.

3   One person puts on the blindfold.

4   Get the person with the blindfold to rest their elbow on the table, holding their hand vertically, like this.

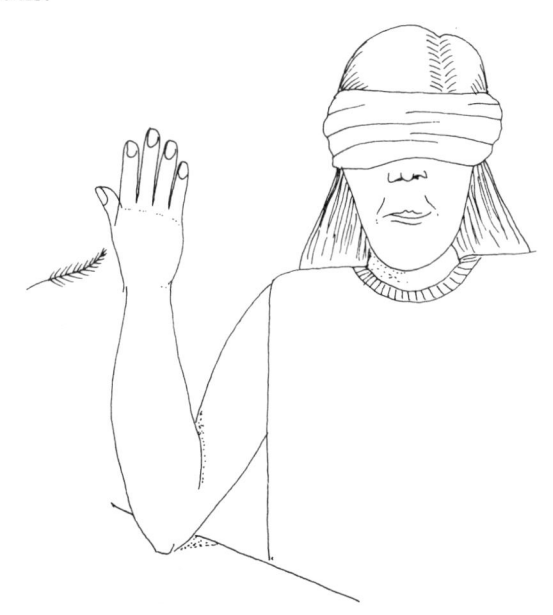

5   Touch various parts of the hand with the feather. Try areas on both the back and the front. Do not have a sequence.

6   Mark 'X's' on the hand outlines when the person could feel the feather.

Think about this
1   Were there some areas where the feather could be felt and others where it could not be felt?

2   Were there any parts of the hands where the feather could be felt more often than others?

3   If there were, perhaps you could suggest why this might be.

Do this
1   Repeat your investigation on various parts of the body.

2   Do not forget to record your results.

Think about this
Were there some parts of the body which were more sensitive than others?

63 a

Assignment Number 64

More About Touch and Feel

P & C We can find out more about touch and feel, and how we come to use our sense of touch and develop it. This happens when we are dealing with familiar objects.

You will need
Notebook, pencil, variety of coins of different denominations, small bag, pair of gloves, a variety of objects with different shapes, blindfold.

Do this
1 You will need to work in twos for this assignment.
2 Blindfold one person.
3 Put the coins into the bag.
4 Give the bag to the blindfolded person.
5 Ask the person to feel and sort out the money.
6 As it is brought out ask him/her to name the coins. Put them in two piles according to whether they are right or wrong.
7 See how effective the assignment was.
8 The blindfolded person could now put on some gloves.
9 Repeat 4, 5 and 6 above.

Think about this
1 Was it easier to discover what the coins were with gloves on or off?
2 Was it easier to discover what the coins were with the blindfold on?
3 If you found it quite easy, why do you think this was?

Primary 5 and 6
Do this
1 Work in twos.
2 One person has to be blindfolded.
3 Give them a variety of familiar objects to feel.
4 Write down those which they get right and those which they get wrong.

Think about this
1 Did you find it easy to identify familiar things without seeing them?
2 Can you explain this?

Do this
1 So far we have only looked at the way we use our hands to feel. We can try it with other parts of the body.
2 Blindfold one person.
3 Give him/her the coins. They do not need to be in a bag this time.
4 Place the coins on the floor, so that the subject can feel them with their toes.

Think about this
1 Was it possible to discover what the coins were using the toes?
2 Was it as easy or as accurate as with the fingers?
3 See if you can think of any reasons to explain any differences.

Find out more
1 See how much you can find out about braille.
2 See whether blind people have developed their sense of feel so that it is better than ours.
3 If you know of a blind person who is willing, you could try some simple investigations like the ones above.

Do this
1 You can play 'Odd Man Out' using feeling/touch.
2 Collect together a number of like objects. These could vary. They could be rough materials to which has been added a smooth one — or vice versa. They could be round ones to which a square one has been added. It depends what you have available.
3 Give the objects to a blindfolded person and ask him to find the odd man out. You might need to give a clue to younger children.

64 a

Assignment Number 65

Discover by Feel

P What we feel with our fingers is very important, but we usually rely on a combination of our senses. To gain an accurate impression we often tend to link what we see with what we feel.

To discover how accurate our sense of touch is, the following investigations are useful. For the investigations to be successful it will be necessary for them to be carried out by two individuals working together.

C At some time you must have put on a blindfold, and tried to discover where things are and what they feel like. It isn't very easy is it? We often forget that we use several of our senses together to give us an accurate picture of the world around us. With this simple investigation you will be able to discover how good your sense of touch is.

You will need
Blindfold, various objects (make sure that they are of different weights, surfaces, etc.) (use pieces of glasspaper, sandpaper, plastic, wood, satin, writing paper, tissue paper, velvet, wood etc), tape recorder, notebook, pencil.

Do this
1. One individual should be blindfolded.
2. The second person passes the objects. You can get the blindfolded person to describe them. What they feel like, how heavy they are, what they are, and so on.
3. Use the tape recorder to record the impressions.
4. Remove the blindfold.

Think about this
1. Each individual should compare what they recorded with the objects.
2. Try to discover whether there are certain parts of the fingers which are more sensitive to touch than others.

Do this
1. If you have a number of people you could carry out this investigation.
2. Blindfold someone.
3. Let them feel the features of someone they know quite well.
4. They should try and discover who it is.
5. Was it easy?

Assignment Number 66

Looking at Eyes

P It is surprising how little we know about parts of our own bodies. Take the eyes for example. Few people, including children, have really looked at them. We might know what colour they are, but we probably know very little else about them.

Members of the same family may or may not have the same coloured eyes. Children might not have the same coloured ones as their parents. On the other hand, if both parents have the same coloured eyes, what colour are the child's? Where parents' eyes are two different colours, are the child's like one of them?

The colour of eyes is something which is decided when sperm and ovum meet at fertilization. Like other body characteristics this information for eye colour is carried in the genes.

C Have you ever looked carefully at your own eyes? Do you know what colour they are? Do you know what colour your parents' eyes are? Are yours like your parents'? You can find out the answers to these questions by looking carefully at eyes.

You will need
Pencil, notebook, mirror, graph paper.

Primary 3 and 4
Do this
1 If you think you know what colour your eyes are, write this down in your notebook.
2 If you know what colours the eyes of the rest of your family are — without looking at them — write this information down as well.
3 Use the mirror to look at your eyes.
4 Draw what you see. Our illustration will help you.

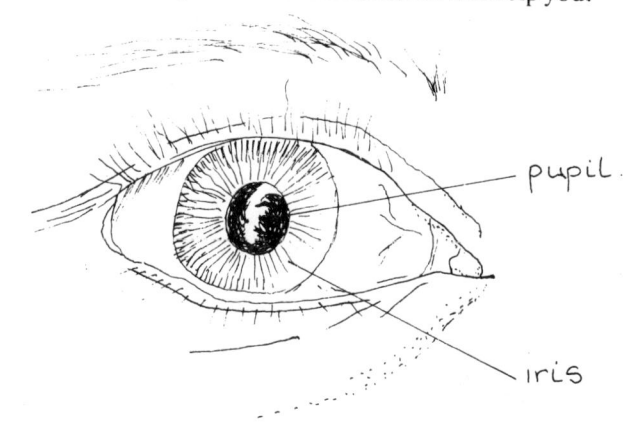

Think about this
1 Did you know what colour your eyes were before you looked at them?
2 Were both your eyes the same colour?
3 Did you know what colour the eyes of the rest of your family were, before you looked at them?
4 Can you see which part of the eye gives it its colour?
5 Look at your parents' eyes. See if you can discover whether yours are like your mother's or your father's.

Primary 5 and 6
Do this
1 Make a list of the colour of as many different people's eyes as possible.
2 When you have collected as much information as you can, plot your results on graph paper.

Think about this
1 Which is the most common eye colour?

Find out more
1 Find out how a camera works. Compare it with your eyes.
2 Which animals have the best eyesight?
3 Which animals have the worst eyesight?

66 a

Assignment Number 67

Looking at Colours

P There are cells in the retina (at the back) of the eye which are able to detect colour. People who are colour blind do not have all of these. These simple investigations will direct attention towards the colours which we see.

C Our eyes are able to pick up colours around us, so that we see things in colour and, not like some animals, in black and white. You can follow the simple instructions to make your own colour spinner, to see how the eye reacts when it does not see colours one at a time. You can also discover something about what happens when one colour passes through another one.

You will need
2 pieces of card about 15 cm x 15 cm, compass (the sort used for drawing circles), string, pencil, ruler, notebook, pointed scissors, torch, coloured paper, glass of water, white paper, oil, mirror.

Do this
1 Cut out a circle as large as possible from one piece of card.

2 You will need to find the middle of the card before you start to draw your circle. See if you can discover how to do this.

3 Look at our diagram, and divide your card up as we have.

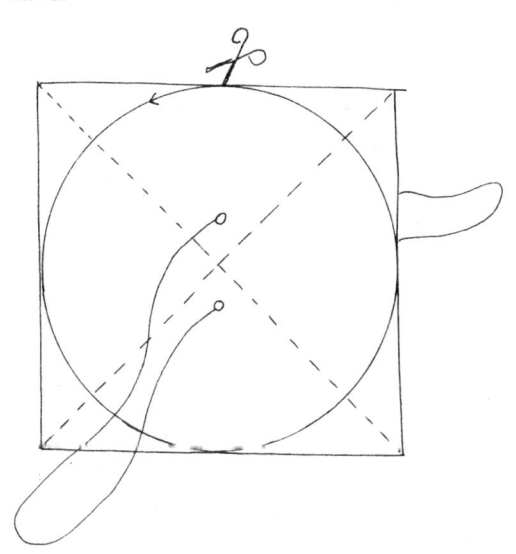

4 Now colour each of the quarters a different colour.

5 Make two holes and thread string or cotton through and tie it so that you can spin the card.

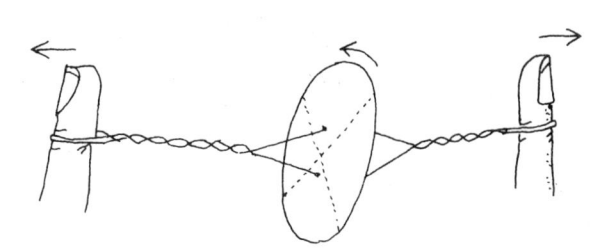

Think about this
1 Discover what happens when you spin the card.

2 Do not forget to write down what you have discovered.

Do this
1 You could make another spinner, using different colours.

Think about this
1 Watch what happens and make notes.

2 Can you explain what is happening?

3 If you have other pieces of card you could experiment with various colour combinations.

Find out more
1 Do you know what the primary colours are?

2 What are the colours of the rainbow?

3 Mix together some colours from your paint box.

Primary 5 and 6
Do this
1 Shine your torch through pieces of coloured paper.

2 Look at the colour of the light before it passes through.

3 What colour was it (a) before it went through and (b) after it went through?

4 Use different coloured papers to investigate what happens.

5 Put one or more pieces of paper together.

You have probably seen a rainbow with all its colours. You can make your own in one of two different ways.

67a

Assignment Number 67

Do this
1   If you have a garden hose with a fine spray you can use this.
2   Wait until the sun is low in the sky.
3   Stand with your back to the sun. If possible make sure that you have something dark to look at.
4   Look through the spray, and describe what you see.

There is an alternative method if you do not have a hose.

Do this
1   Fill a tumbler with water.
2   Place it on a window sill when the sun is shining brightly.
3   Hold a sheet of plain white paper below the level of the window sill. You may need to tilt your tumbler.

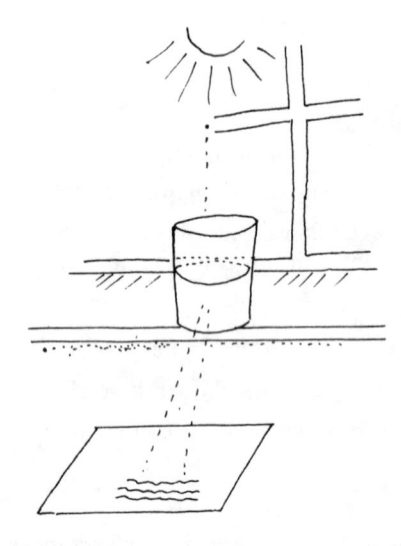

Think about this
1   What can you see on your paper?

Find out more
1   When do you see rainbows?

Do this
1   Put a drop of oil from a small can into a puddle of water.
2   Can you see anything?
3   Can you explain it?
4   Use a paper towel or other absorbent material to mop up the oil and the puddle after your experiment. Why do you think you should do this?

Seeing Colours

P & C Unless we are all colour blind, we see a variety of colours. We have looked at these when we tried Assignment Number 67 about rainbows.

Have you ever wondered whether we see all colours as easily? Have you ever thought that some colours might be picked up more easily by the eye than others?

This simple Assignment will help you to discover something about this aspect of seeing colours.

You will need
Six different coloured pencils, notebook, pencil.

Do this
1 Work in twos for this Assignment.
2 Mark a dot in the centre of a clean page in your notebook.
3 Now arrange for one person to look at the dot. Their eyes should be about 15 cm from the paper.
4 Close one eye.
5 Bring the pencils towards the dot from various angles.
6 Try one colour at a time and all colours in turn.
7 As soon as the person can tell the colour of the pencil, mark a small 'x' on the paper.
8 Repeat this until you have at least four 'x's' for each colour. Although we cannot show you colour, we can show you the idea.

Think about this
1 Were some colours seen more easily than others?
2 Was there any difference between the eyes?

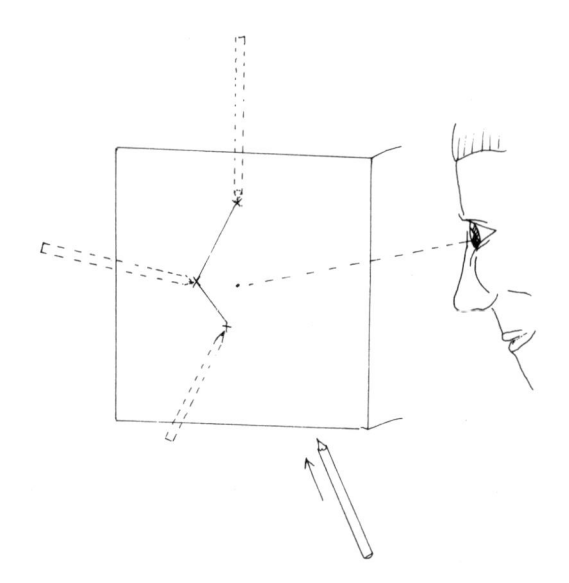

9 Join up the dots.
10 Repeat with the other eye.
11 Change places and repeat the Assignment.
12 Use other people so that you can repeat this.

Assignment Number 69

Do Our Eyes Deceive Us? (1)

P & C We rely on our senses to tell us all sorts of things which are happening around us. We rely on our eyes very much. But is the information which we get always accurate? We can discover whether this is so, by carrying out the following investigation.

You will need
Notebook, pencil, illustrations shown here.

Do this
1 Look at each of the diagrams and answer the questions which appear underneath.

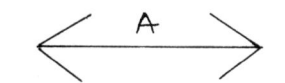

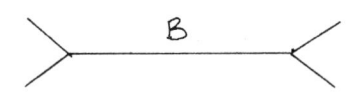

Think about this
1 When you looked at the optical illusions, did you find that there were times when the brain didn't always tell the truth?

2 Do you think there might be times when we receive wrong information which might be harmful?

3 We call these illustrations optical illusions.

Which is longer A or B?

STOP AT THE THE KERB.

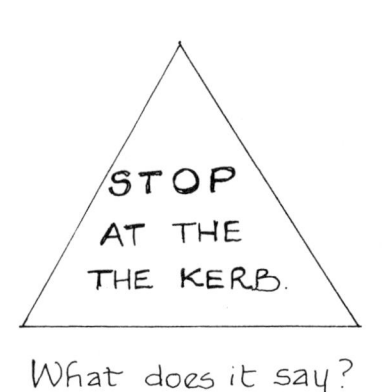

What does it say?

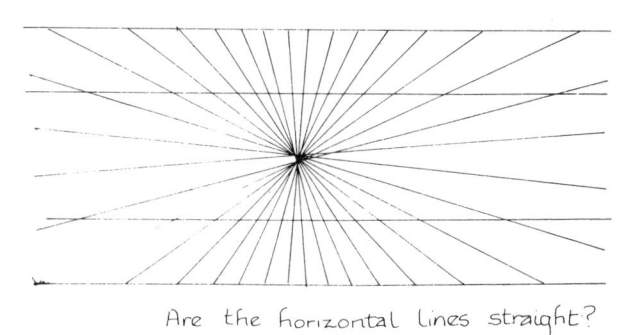

Are the horizontal lines straight?

69 a

Assignment Number 70

Do Our Eyes Deceive Us? (2)

P & C Our eyes sometimes deceive us (see also Assignment sheet 69), and these suggestions will help to illustrate this.

You will need
Piece of card about 6 cm x 10 cm, strong cotton, pair of scissors, pencil, notebook.

Do this
1 Draw a square 4 cm x 4 cm in the centre of each side of the card.

2 Draw (or trace) a picture of a lion on one side of the card — in the centre square.

3 Draw (or trace) a picture of a cage on the other side of the card — in the centre square.

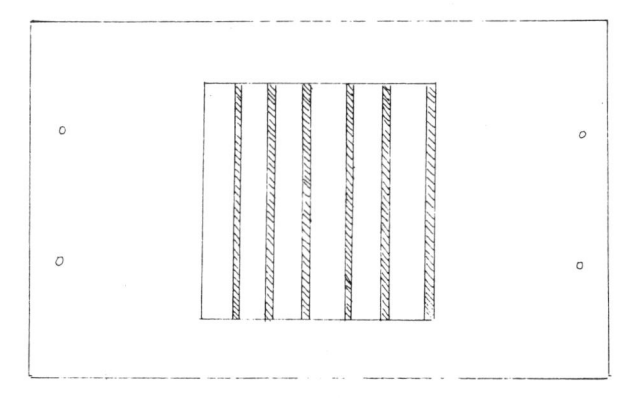

4 Make a cotton loop at the top and bottom of the card.

5 Put your finger in each loop, and then wind up the card.

6 Once the cotton is wound up, let it go so that the card spins freely.

Think about this
1 What did you see as the card was spinning? Did you see a lion and a cage, or a lion in a cage?

2 If you saw the lion in the cage, why do you think this was?

Find out more
1 Find out how a movie camera works to produce moving pictures.

70 a

Assignment Number 71

How Our Eyes Work

You will need
Pencil, piece of paper, mirror.

Do this
1 Hold one of your fingers up.
2 Shut one eye.
3 Look at the finger with the open eye.

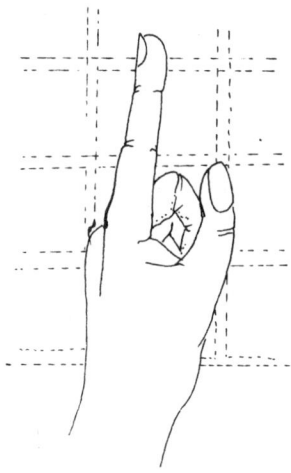

4 Can you also see the things in the distance — without moving your focus from your finger?

Think about this
Which did you see most clearly, the finger or the distant objects?

Do this
Now, without moving your head or your eyes, focus on something in the distance.

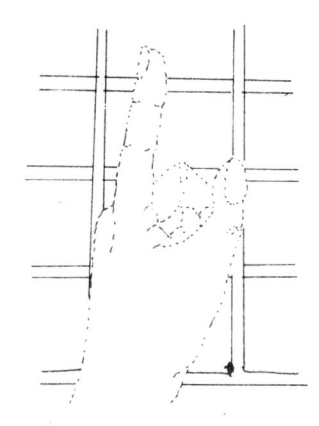

Think about this
1 Did you notice anything happening?
2 Can you explain it?

Do this
1 Stand facing another person.
2 Hold a pencil about 5 cm in front of their eyes.
3 Look at his eyes.
4 Now tell him to look at the pencil.
5 Now tell him to look beyond you.

Think about this
1 What did you notice happening?
2 Can you explain it?

Do this
1 Use your pencil to draw a dot on a piece of paper.
2 Stand up, and place the piece of paper on the table.
3 Close one eye and bring your pencil point **quickly** onto the dot, so that it makes a mark — wherever you hit.
4 Open this eye, and close the other one.
5 Bring the pencil down onto the dot, **quickly,** so that it makes a mark.
6 Open both eyes, and bring the pencil point down onto the dot.

Think about this
1 Did you manage to bring the point down onto the dot when your right eye was shut?
2 Did you manage to bring the point down onto the dot when your left eye was shut?
3 Did you manage to bring your pencil point down onto the dot when both eyes were open?
4 Which was the easiest?
5 How far away were the other marks?
6 Why do you think that two eyes are better than one?

Primary 5 and 6
Do this
1 Hold a pencil at arm's length in line with the upright on a window.
2 Now close the left eye.

Think about this
Did you notice anything happening when you closed your eye?

Do this
Repeat with the other eye closed.

Think about this
1 Did you notice anything happening this time?
2 Can you explain what happened?

71 a

The Use of Lenses

P We have lenses in our eyes, and we find artificial lenses in all sorts of places. They are in binoculars, spectacles, telescopes and cameras.

Primary 3 and 4 will need to be told where these are, whereas Primary 5 and 6 will be able to make a list.

We have indicated which of these investigations can be carried out by Primary 3 and 4 and those suitable for Primary 5 and 6. You will need to explain the differences between convex lenses and concave ones.

C There are different kinds of lenses. If you have a pair of spectacles you can feel these. It may be that other members of your family also wear spectacles. Look at the lenses to see if they are all the same. If you have an old camera you can feel the lens in this as well. See if you can compare it with the lenses in the spectacles.

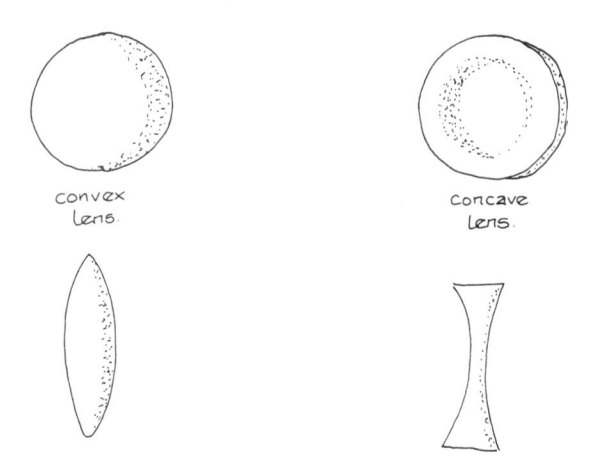

convex lens.

concave lens.

You will need
Convex lens, sheet of paper, notebook, pencil.

Do this
1 One person needs to hold the lens vertically.
2 He should be facing a window.
3 A second person needs to place the sheet of white paper vertically behind the lens. 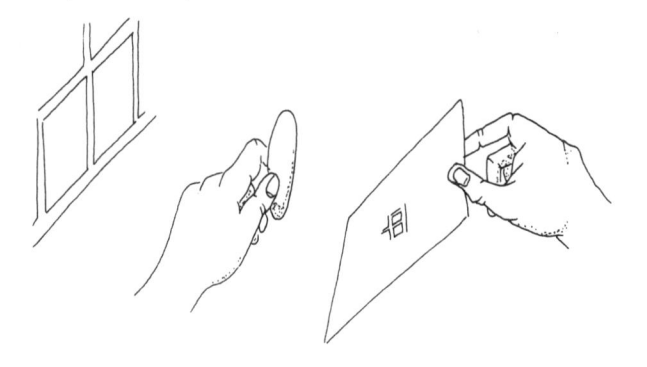
4 Experiment with the lens by moving it backwards and forwards.
5 Stop when there is a sharp inverted (upside down) image of the scene outside the window on the white paper.

Think about this
1 Why did the image appear upside down?
2 Why don't we see things upside down, even though we have a convex lens in the eye?

Find out more
Primary 5 and 6
1 How do you think it might be possible to turn the image on the white paper the right way up?
2 Can you make a list of the sorts of places where you might expect to find lenses.
3 Can you find out what sort of lenses people need in their glasses if they are (a) long-sighted and (b) short-sighted?

Assignment Number 73

Making a Flickergraph

P & C When you flick through a number of in-sequence pictures quickly they appear to be moving. This happens when we watch a film on television. You can discover whether this is true by making a flickergraph.

You will need
Notebook, pencil, a few pieces of plain paper size 10 cm x 10 cm, paper clip or stapler.

Do this
1 Draw something or somebody going through an action. It might be a jack in the box, or a bird opening and shutting its beak.

2 We have drawn an example for you to look at.

3 Draw one picture on each piece of paper to show the action.

73 a

Assignment Number 73

3 Fix the pictures into a small book. The first picture in the sequence should be at the back and the last one at the front.

4 Fix all the pages together. Do this with a paper clip or stapler.

5 Flick through the pictures from back to front.

Think about this
1 What did you notice as you flicked through the pages.

2 Why do you think this happened?

Do this
1 Try flicking through the pictures at **different** speeds.

2 What did you notice?

Discovering Tongue Taste Areas

P & C When exploring on the walk, we use four of our five senses regularly — hearing, seeing, touching/feeling and smelling. We seldom use taste on our walk. Yet this is very important. Our ancestors knew how important it was. When they lived nomadic lives they had to taste wild fruits and berries to see whether they were edible and palatable. Wild animals still do this.

Humans still rely on a sense of taste, but most of the time it is to tell us whether we like something or whether we do not like it. We all have the same sorts of taste buds, and yet some people like sour things: other people do not.

Our taste also tells us when foods which we eat 'do not taste quite right' — we can usually tell when something is slightly off, or going bad.

Most people do not realise that we can only distinguish four different tastes. All the things which we eat are made up of these four. With the following investigations, we can discover something about our sense of taste.

You will need
Solutions of salt, sugar (sweet), quinine sulphate or lemon (bitter) and acetic acid or vinegar (sour), drinking straws, four small containers, blindfold, notebook, pencil, labels, mirror.

Do this
1 Make up weak solutions of salt, sugar, quinine sulphate or lemon and acetic acid or vinegar.

2 Flatten one end of the straws before you use them.

3 Label the containers — sweet, sour, bitter and salt.

4 Draw a tongue outline in your book, using your own tongue as a guide. Look in a mirror. We have drawn one to help you.

5 Put a straw in each beaker. Make sure you replace them in the correct beakers.

6 Blindfold the subject.

7 Using the straw, drop a spot of each solution — one at a time — on different parts of the subject's tongue. Try to ensure that it is a small drop so that it does not spread across the tongue.

8 Use the following symbols — a for salt; b for sweet; c for bitter and d for sour. Record the area on the tongue where the liquid could actually be tasted.

9 When the subject tells you **correctly** what the taste was use the appropriate letter on the appropriate part of the tongue drawing. If the subject is incorrect, do not mark anything on the chart.

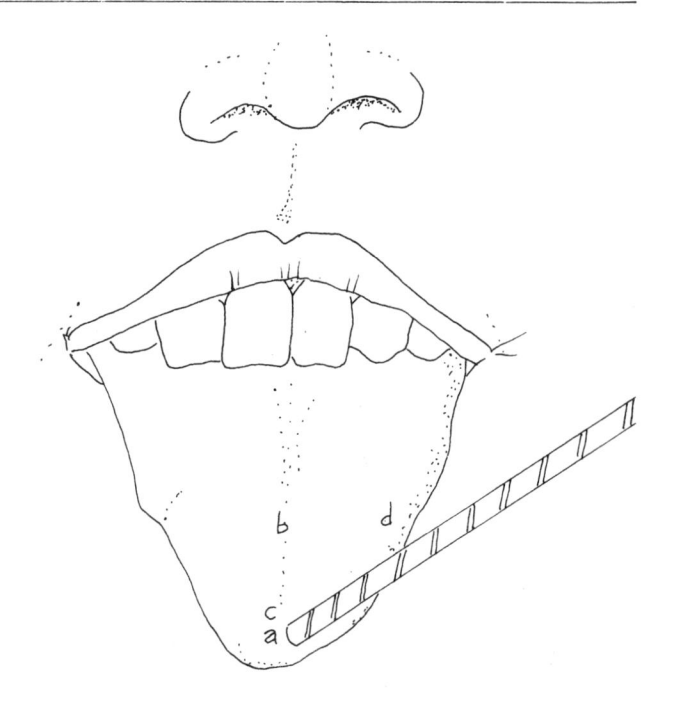

10 Continue to do this until the whole area of the tongue has been tested with all the solutions.

11 Vary the solution and the sequence.

12 You could repeat the investigation, with the subjects changing places.

13 When you have finished look at the tongue drawing together.

Think about this
1 Is it possible to distinguish different tastes all over the tongue? For example, do you taste salt on every part of the tongue.

2 Do you have areas on the tongue(s) where some things can be tasted but not others?

3 Do you think it is really necessary to taste all food over the whole of your tongue? Think about what happens when you eat your food and this should help you with your answer.

Find out more
1 Make a list of all the food you eat in a day. Decide whether each tastes sweet, sour, bitter or salt.

Assignment Number 75

Taste and Smell

Our senses of taste and smell are closely linked. We can discover whether this is so by a simple experiment.

You will need
Onion, apple, knife, three small dishes or saucers, blindfold, peg, notebook, pencil.

Do this
1 Cut a number of small cubes from the apple. Place them in one of the dishes.

2 Peel the onion. Squeeze the juice from it into the other dish.

3 You can stop your eyes from watering when you peel the onion, by doing it under water.

4 Soak half the apple cubes in the onion juice. Place them in a separate dish.

5 You need two people. One should be blindfolded.

6 Place the peg on the child's nose.

7 Put a piece of plain apple on your child's tongue.

8 When you have completed steps 2 and 3 in **Do This** (see above), place the apple, soaked in onion, on your child's tongue.

9 You can repeat the process so that your child can test you.

10 Record the result in your notebook.

11 When you placed the apple on your child's tongue, what did he/she taste? You should keep records of the replies in a small notebook.

12 When you placed the apple soaked in onion juice on the tongue what could the subject taste? Record the replies in the notebook.

13 If the subject still said 'apple' could be tasted, take the peg off the nose.

Think about this
1 What was he/she able to taste when the peg was removed?

2 Was the subject really tasting when the peg was removed?

3 How did the subject know that it was onion?

4 What other sense is closely connected with taste?

75 a

Assignment Number 76

Smell Without Seeing

P To try to discover how good our sense of smell is we can use 'substances' which are familiar but which we cannot see, because the containers which they are in are covered up.

Have six or eight small containers of the same size. Cover the outside with paper if they are glass. Once the 'substances' are inside, cover the top with muslin.

You could use any common 'substances'. For example you might try coffee, grass, tea, onion, toothpaste, banana, etc.

C How well do you recognise common smells when you do not actually see where they come from. This investigation will help you to discover whether your sense of smell is very accurate.

You will need
The small containers which have the 'smells' in them, notebook, pencil.

Do this
1 Write numbers in your notebook — corresponding to the numbers on the small containers.

2 Smell Number 1.

3 Write down what you think it is.

4 Smell number 2, and so on.

5 Write down what you think each smell was.

Think about this
1 Look at your results. See how many you got right.

2 How efficient do you think your own sense of smell is?

Find out more
1 We all like pleasant smells. Make a list of things which smell nice in and around the house.

2 Can you think of any harmful substances which if we could not smell them, would be dangerous.

3 Can you discover which animals have a very good sense of smell?

4 Find out what police dogs are used for. How do you think smell is important to these animals?

Assignment Number 77

Looking at Different Faces

P We know that every mouse is a mouse because it looks like all other mice we know. We know which plants are clover, because we know what a clover plant looks like. We recognise human beings because we know what they look like. We can pick out our relatives from a crowd of people because we recognise their faces. We know one relative from another because they have variations.

Variations occur at fertilization because the sperm (male cell) and ovum (female cell) carry these. Some characteristics come from the female and some from the male.

These investigations will help us to appreciate something about some of our differences.

C You can always recognise one of your relatives from another because they look different. Although they have many things in common — ears, eyes, nose, mouth, and so on — all these are slightly different so that everyone is unique. We can carry out some simple studies to discover more about some of our differences.

You will need
Light source (e.g. anglepoise, table lamp, or torch with strong beam), darkened corner, chair, sheets of plain paper, pencil.

Do this
1. Darken a room, or a corner of a room.
2. Plug in the lamp.
3. Put the chair near a wall.
4. Sit in the chair.
5. Look forward.
6. Eyes should be closed.
7. Shine the light on the side of the face. This produces a shadow on the wall.
8. Draw around the outline of the shadow carefully.
9. Change places and repeat the above.
10. If possible repeat with (a) other members of the family and (b) other people.

Think about this
1. Did you see a difference between the outlines?
2. If you did what were the differences? You could cut out the shapes.
3. Did members of the same family have any features which looked similar — e.g. nose, forehead, chin, etc.
4. Give the silhouettes to other people and see if they can tell which one belongs to which person.

Assignment Number 78

Looking at Differences — Fingerprints

P Most people realise that one of the easiest ways of catching criminals is to match their fingerprints against those found at the scene of the crime — supposing of course that they left any.

We are all different, although members of the same family may have similarities. The fingerprint investigation is something which, with a little practice, can be carried out, and enjoyed by almost anyone. It soon shows up the differences. It is suggested that the fingerprints of as many people as possible are collected. Try to keep prints of members of the same family close together, so that children can compare them.

C Everyone has a different set of fingerprints, and this is one way of showing our differences. You may have noticed others. Although you may look like your parents — perhaps you have some things which are like dad and some which are like mum — you are different from them. The fingerprint is one such difference which we can easily show.

You will need
An ink pad if possible (otherwise use a piece of blotting paper soaked with ink, if using this method, put it in some kind of tray to prevent too much mess), plain sheets of paper, notebook, pencil.

Do this
1 You will find that getting a clear impression of your fingerprint often needs some practice, so don't give up if you get smudged or imperfect ones the first few times.

2 Take fingerprints from all fingers on both hands, taking care to label which fingers they came from.

3 Roll the finger on the inked surface.

4 Place the inked finger on a clean sheet of paper, and press from side to side.

Think about this
1 Fingerprints fall into one of eight types according to the way in which they are formed. Look at yours and compare them with the illustrations.

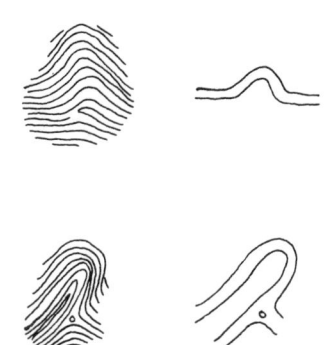

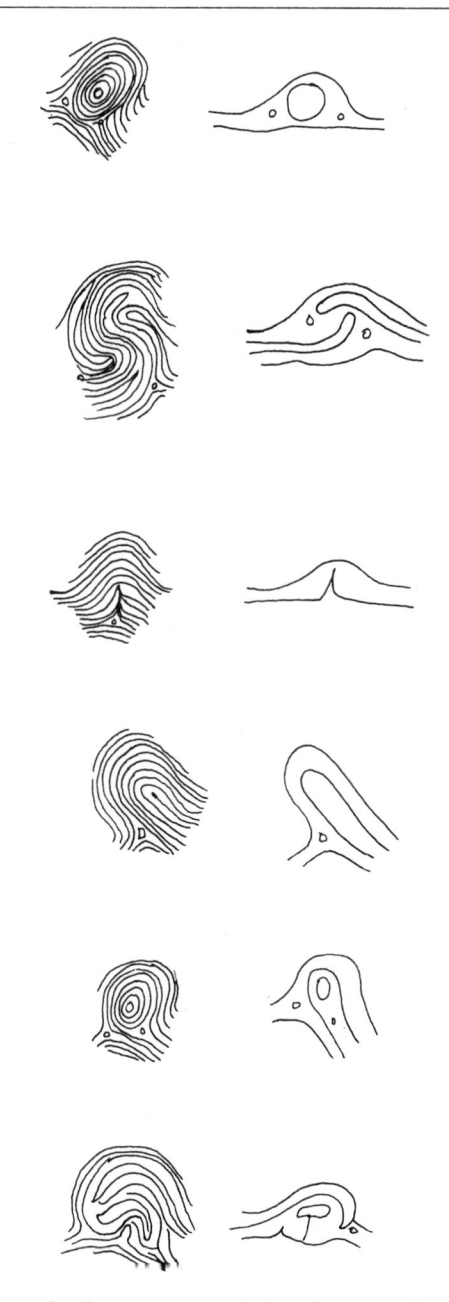

2 See whether you — and the other people whose fingerprints you take — have variations on the same and different hands.

3 You wll be able to classify the fingerprints, according to the eight types if you can collect a large number, although this might not be possible.

4 Perhaps you will be able to see whether some occur more frequently than others.

5 When you have a good collection, see how easy (or how difficult) it is to spot the differences.